40 DAYS AND 40 NIGHTS
WITHIN THE SHED IN THE WOODS

By Tracy Pringle

Edited by Anuradha Kapoor

Cover by Malhar Tanna

Published by Outliers Publishing Pvt. Ltd.

First Edition 2019

ISBN: 978-81-935692-7-6

EDITOR'S PROFILE

After the age of 40 I discovered my passion for writing which led me to become a freelance author, blogger, content writer and editor. I am proud to be one of the top bloggers on momspresso, where I have written more than 100 blogs. Having written around 25 short stories till date, I have published a book by the name of 'Stories from the heart's which is a compilation of 22 short stories. I was recently awarded by the Indian Awaz for being an inspirational author in the year 2018, title of Influential author by The Spiritmania and the prestigious Swami Vivekananda Award for Excellence in literature. I have conducted various blogging and story writing workshops for adults and children and have also edited a few books for Indian as well as overseas authors.

My Facebook Profile:
https://www.facebook.com/anuradha.kapoor.35

~Anuradha Kapoor, Editor

PREFACE

A big thank you to all my friends, teachers and family who have supported me along this journey and to the Garden Station Langley on Tyne, for honouring my calling… for the 40 days and 40 nights living in silence alone, 'Within' The Shed In the woods.

I remember the time when I had started to clear the shed, ready for my arrival, the hundreds of mouse droppings that needed to be taken out, the holes in the panels and the bunch of newspapers that I shredded to make paper mache.

As I pressed it all into the corners of any holes that were big enough to let rodents in, I prayed for assistance that they would not nibble through into the space, my space for the next six weeks, and how the fabric blew back and forth as I placed it on the sides as the wind came blowing through.

The holes were many and the leaning of the shed to one side great, but what else did I expect as you had explained that it was now 200 years old.

200… I could not believe it but as you had mentioned, it had previously been a plater man's shed where pieces of the train lines were initially kept.

No wonder I said I keep seeing the energy of a man here…he looks like a signalman watching us as we go around our business.

As long as he leaves me in peace during the six weeks, I think to myself…what an adventure, this is already turning out to be. I thank you so much, for without your kindness and help, I know this book and 'The One Road' would have never been completed, so I am eternally grateful for I realize how blessed I am.

There have been many special friends along the way, who have supported me and I am unable to name you all but you know in your hearts who you are... for I love you so much and I have told you so, as we are all here to support each other on our own individual paths.

God did not create the jealousy feature for this beautiful world, we did, in our own free will, so we should stay in our wisdom and knowledge that we are all born equal and we all have the same opportunity to find out the truth.

This book has been written throughout the 40 days and 40 nights as I have listened to my inner wisdom, the whisperings of my soul and completed yet another part of my calling. I have been meditating during this time and allowing the thoughts, the messages and my intuition to flow... as I listen intuitively to the inner promptings in the silence, for the silence speaks so loudly.

The connection with nature has also assisted me in bringing this book and 'The One Road' into fruition as understood through my own experience.

I hope you enjoy its contents and that you too can perhaps begin to do your own soul searching for the truth. For as I have walked my path, especially this last two years, I can genuinely say nothing has been more rewarding. It has had its challenges as after all, I am just a soul signature having a human experience, in this reality in the here and now. I love you always...my children, grandchild, and all my friends, past and present, and I still want what's best for you as I hold you all dear in my heart.

Without you I can survive, as I know there is not really any separation in the one consciousness, but I would never have made it thus far without you…

Please remember to always love each other, and that kindness is magical.

Always be the student and the teacher…as we share in the one love, the peace, the joy and with all the blessings, be the hope for the world and shine your light brightly for you can make a difference, for you are never alone, no matter what the appearances may be.

A special thank you to Louis and to Mack, for I know you both saw within me… a long time before I did, so I bless you both so very very much.

Love and Blessings

Always X

INTRODUCTION

It is funny how I am writing the introduction at the end. I think this has occurred because I did not realize the true significance of it all, in the beginning. But now although I am at the end, it is not really the end. For now, this is the start… the new beginning, the new chapter and maybe even the start of book three. For, I did not realise just how much my life would change by this experience and the personal growth that would occur so rapidly.

As I look back now to my time in Essex only six weeks ago. I was not ready to come back up north, for my heart was still in an area where I had made so many friends, over the past twelve months of living there. I felt I had been ripped away, from the bosom of somewhere that I now called home, yet previously Northumberland had been my home too and I had loved it with all my heart. The last day of my working week down south, my shamanic teachers had said they felt that I needed to do the Ascended Masters meditation. For they were receiving guidance on my behalf and I had felt that too, for it had been pulling at my heart all week. It felt like there was a sense of urgency but as time was running out, Nick said I will do it with you to make sure it's done because it's important as he could feel it too. So off we go together to a quiet place, and as we start to go within, it was during this that it became so clear.

It was like a vision and a calling for I was being told, for it said I must not return home. At first, I was surprised for I thought I have to go back, but as the message was reinforced with such strength, I knew it was true. I must not, under any circumstances return to my daughter's home, and I had a feeling that I would never live their again, but I did not to know why, how or where I would be.

Then they proceeded to tell me that I had to do a period of silence, a hermitage of 40 days and 40 nights within the wilderness. For some reason…Something…I don't know why, but I just accepted it. I accepted it in total trust for I did not know why or where this period of silence could take place, but I knew in my heart that it would.

For the first time in my life, it was total surrender, no question or doubt entered my mind, for I knew it would be alright. I informed my teachers afterwards and they looked surprised but I had already sent the message ahead, to where I thought it could possibly be as I went with my gut instincts and waited. The following morning, the reply came through "Yes that is ok, we will honour your calling," and it was from there that it all began, as in a haze, within a few days it was all set to go.

The adventure "within" as I truly got to 'Know Thyself Well', little did I know that a book was about to be born. This book, for that, was never in the equation. I had thought about writing a follow on book, from my first, 'Letters from the Heart' that had birthed after the death of my son.

But it had not been written, for life such as the death of my father and a divorce got in the way and not a word had appeared on paper. Yet as soon as I went into silence, it shot through, as inspired writing… and I knew, that another chapter in my life was taking shape. Then came the principles…'The One Road' - The 21 basic principles for the living, after a walk in the wood, I had to rush for paper and a pen because I could not stop the flow of words. Next came along 'A Mission Statement' and as I viewed it all, I now realize that this has been trapped, trapped within me… for a very long time. Now as I speak to a publisher, a radio, a newspaper, and TV, I am wondering how far this will travel.

I realise just how significant this has been for me and not just for me and my family, but for many others. For I really hope it helps someone else in some way, my experiences as they have been shown, my vision and my journey. For if it can help one, and then it can help thousands, for I know how the love spreads. It is as infectious as any disease and so much better for you too, for so much joy and love there is to be had and to be shared. As I now say, do not worry for all we need to do is to change everything there is about ourselves. Oh no I hear the groans as I laugh, for we are comfortable in our version of the safe and the familiar.

Yet in change, these are the greatest gifts of discovery if we are brave enough to take the first step. How many of us quit... just before the miracle occurs? And how many would stop turning over the plant pots, if they knew for sure a million pounds was hiding under just one. But people do because they are ingrained in their habits, beliefs, and attitudes... I know because mine have been. Yet something within me from very small, always knew that the fear of a living death, of staying the same, in the same old was somehow far worse than the risk of stepping out into the unknown. For just around that corner, just a few more steps, there may be a view, a view that you have never seen, that can and will take your breath away like never before! So, I did not turn back, I kept on and on, in the hope and the faith and the trust that one day I would eventually find it.

Like a great explorer, I carried on against the odds, the jeers from friends and sometimes family, for I can still hear those words. 'You are mad!' Sometimes you have to believe in yourself more than others believe in you... and if you do, one day I can assure you it will be found- Your Liquid Gold.

Enjoy this book with an open mind and an open heart and if it does not resonate at this time, put it down, but do not discard it. Look again from time to time, for you may not be ready just now, as I once was not but then as I read again, I was suddenly ready to receive...the truth.

All my love and all my blessings for your continued journey and may you all find your happiness within.

Always Tracy XXX

DAY 1

As I start my 40 days and 40 nights, I decided to start a ceremony in honour of the Ascended Masters and the Earth. I initially kneel at the statue of the Buddha in the garden. Saying a prayer and scattering seeds in all the directions North, South, East and West as my son suddenly shoots in with a message. "When at the shed, feed the birds, feed them daily and do not forget." As I return inside and light a candle with Sandalwood Incense for stability and integrity, only a very small flame begins…then both the incense and the candle go out together in sync; so I find another one and this time they both light fully.

MESSAGE

It starts with a small flame in the hearts of the people, you light it, and then it will grow in love. Eat, Drink, Walk and Speak mindfully, be grateful and see the Grace in all things visible and invisible. After 40 days, speak of your experiences as there will be many. Number 9 is significant as this is a magic number; it is of high vibration and on the 9th day… takes note of everything that occurs around you; for there may be something. As I study that evening, as instructed by the life of Jesus, Buddha and St Francis the 9th day jumps out at me as Jesus was betrayed on the 9th day. The owner of the Garden Station had messaged me to say that they have named their new puppy Wolfe… How apt I thought, as they do not know, but my shamanic power animal is a wolf… plus dogs are the representation of unconditional love, for DOG spelt backwards is GOD.

With that my sheet of affirmations shoots out of the back of my journal from 2018 and as I gaze over the words; I realise that I am in the manifestation of these words right now. The word Presence…jumps out at me, how funny as an Indian lady at the garage suddenly said you are a… something? She felt my energy… Lol, what next! My feeling is that I am being led into the40 days and 40 nights gently from my sanctuary, within the barn and onto the shed in the woods.

MESSAGE

Your journal is to become your friend… On Bank Holiday i.e. Monday, speak of your experiences and remember the book, The Magic Faraway Tree that you read as a child… (I had forgotten) The upside-down world of topsy-turvy and how everything this last 2 years has tipped upside down… The comparison, the adventures, and how the Love and Pain have lit the flame of unconditional love in your heart! For everything is connected… From a stone to a blade of grass, a plant, animal, bird, child, adult, divinity, stars, universe to the counsels of 9 and 13 for those who understand. Everything is beauty.

Yet in the blink of an eye, it is missed. It is an illusion, like a sleepy spell that people choose to live under. Like sleeping beauty… yet love can set you free. The truth of unconditional love.

You are not free with karmic relationships but the purity of real love needs to be discovered, the depth of which you feel in your heart like no other. As I sit listening to the chirping of the birds and the blowing of the wind, I can feel the whirring sensation deep within my physical body, the Universe within; as it turns and flows.

My heart starts to pound wildly as I clear my mind to emptiness… nothingness but Peace, Love and Connection, the depth of which cannot be told for it has to be "experienced."

15

As I shower, I surrender to the moment of the water as I merge with the flow and allow it to cascade over my naked body, seeing its beauty and connection to all things. I was born naked and I will leave this planet naked, stripped bare of all things material. I cannot take anything with me, but the great love of Grace that will reside within my heart energy; that endless, deep vibration of the OM, the hum of peace, the universal God of Love. Such is my gratitude, for I am so grateful. The Universe is friendly to me!

10:45 - A noticing occurs. Why does it seem that there are so many things to do all of sudden?
Breakfast Tick
Washing up Tick
Laundry Tick
Dogs fed and walked Tick Tick

Distractions... Slow down and breathe... The material world tries to intervene and time is part of the illusion. Back to basics. Refocus and only do what is necessary. The mind then tries to jump ahead to the weekend, friends, work, chemist, etc.
STOP... Discipline... I pull myself to a halt...

Living in the NOW
I only have this second for there is no getting back on that hamster wheel, for the world will turn with or without me.

11:10 - I remember the doorways that I have passed through already - 1, 2 10?Did I even notice? Did I walk through the door into the garden in consciousness? Or had I returned to my sleep state my slumber?

MESSAGE

It is no good being a Prince or a Princess if you cannot be a noble pauper. Listen to the wind, to the whisperings of the Universe. My inner garden comes into my awareness, the weeding of any negativity that no longer serves me; plant the good seeds only and allow the fruits to bear.

11:50 - What do I actually need at this moment... as Swami instructed me. Listen to the body he said and fulfill its needs. As I breathe slowly in and out in a relaxed state. The body is thirsty. Drink... I savour each mouthful of the tea I have just prepared; the spoon in the cup suddenly seems as loud as it clangs on the side of the china. This silence is deafening!!!

As I gaze out of the window, a noticing occurs again. Were those daffodils that yellow? Was that Buddha smiling? The grass is so green and the birds so loud. Hmm... back to the sweet tea nectar... I can hear every sound.

Even the sound of my swallowing and the feeling of the liquid as it travels through the body, it is like watching myself in action. Even as I write this in my journal, I am observing my hand and the pen. The hearts thuds for there is the hum of the deep peace within, which appears to fall deeper than it was before. Suddenly, the mind jumps to a memory of a train and staring into the eyes of a friend, as we merge in this stillness the train appears to disappear. As I hear my voice... it says in reply you call it nothingness but I call it sacred space as it merges into the Universe.

The train stops... time to get off!

12:50 - Waiting for a bus. Suddenly an obtrusive thought flashes into my mind. So why did you leave?

MESSAGE

Relationships are not hard. They are born of effective communication and unconditional love. As I get on to the bus and ask for my ticket I turn to the right and a sudden jolt of JOY hits my heart. A wonderful surprise… for my youngest daughter is sitting there. My heart swells with love for Clio is one of my special children, now 17 years of age. All grown up with a new job, a soon to be home of her own and a boyfriend in town. How things have changed and how life moves on, as we are all finding our authentic way out of our self-made prisons and into the light. She asks me, "Have you started your 40 days and 40 nights yet?"

Yes, I reply, but I do not go into my secret location to sleep for another couple of days. However, I am already in practice, study, meditation, discipline, etc. Clio smiles as I get up to leave the bus. I hug her and kiss her goodbye and I can almost hear her thoughts. But here are mine, my child…for I am the blessed one. Blessed to have been your mother, for you have brought me so much joy and taught me so much already. Always the student and the teacher! May God bless you, for you have endured so much already in your short life; yet you remain such a beautiful soul with a heart full of nothing but love.

1:10 - During the walk to my location, I notice a gate to a tiny garden. The garden has a bench in the centre, which is surrounded by daffodils. I look around for a house and soon realise it is a public garden, a hidden one off the road with a little place to sit. How wonderful I think, as this is a gem of a discovery and a lovely place to sit in nature… to contemplate.

THE SHED IN THE WOODS...

My home until Easter Monday. My heart is filled with gratitude, as I throw rugs down on the linoleum covered floor. I am setting up my tiny house and I think to myself this is not hardship... this is luxury. Look how lucky I am... I have an electric socket for my lamp so I can study. I have an extension for a heater for warmth. I have access to water and a toilet... goodness I am truly blessed. For if I were homeless, this would be a mansion fit for a princess, this is the Ritz! The excitement fills me as I hear the birds, "Don't worry" I say "I hear you. I will feed you every day and we will become friends."

As I breathe in the fresh air, I can hear nothing but nature and the hum of the OM within. Deep, deep peace. Thought of a previous home shoots in 4 bedrooms all en suite, how lucky I was. A thought crosses my mind, but what did I actually need it all for? Because now as I look around me at the bigger picture. I can see it. I am truly blessed. The Universe is friendly to me and I am so grateful.

7:00 - Study time... As I study the lives of Jesus, St Francis and Buddha...

I wonder...were they not just all part of the same ONE energy.

MESSAGE
Know Thyself Well...How many times have I heard this? Thoughts creep in... What am I? Define your product. I am the product. I am an Author Spiritual Teacher and a Healer. I heal with both the written and the spoken word, as I touch the hearts and minds of people with love. I also heal with my hands as I am a conduit for the energy... AMAZING. Huh, Simple Lol... Laughter and Love really is the best medicine! All that looking in the mirror and affirming to

myself I love you has obviously worked. All that peeling away of the layers of the onion; as the fears have surfaced, I have thrown them into the visionary white flame to burn away, all that no longer serves me. Over and over again, ridding myself of all the pain. For as the saying goes no pain no gain. I am released from suffering, to live in Joy, Peace and Love.

Thinking of burning a thought occurs as I look down at my feet both of which were burnt last week; when I dropped a kettle of boiling water on them. I lovingly cream the right one, with Calendula and Comfrey and I notice the red scars look like rope burns; wrapped around my foot. It is as if I have been bound or tethered in some way. Symbolically maybe, as I had allowed myself to be held back perhaps. The Left is nearly healed too but that looks like it has been pierced very weirdly indeed... Does it matter? No not in the slightest, as my relationship with my body is healed; I am beautiful both inside and out. My soul signature finally knows that part well.

9:00 - Time for bed and as I listen to the silence, the feeling of the hum that I know so well; my physical body needs to rest. I go to move but sudden dizziness occurs like vertigo; but I know it is not... for it is a feeling I have studied. I do wonder if it is the nervous system, as it realigns to the change in the energy; for it is like the density of the physical body appears lighter.

With that, I remember a physics lesson at university when the lecturer tapped a table and said, 'You think this is solid, don't you?"

"It is not", he said. It is just that the molecules are more tightly packed together, so it gives the appearance of being solid. Lol, as I shake my head... it is an illusion. Goodnight and may your God

Bless you whoever that may be for you. Buddha, Jesus, Ganesh, it doesn't really matter, just allow the blessings to flow into your life and enjoy.

10:15- I had fallen asleep instantly but was woken to a dream and what appears to be unpleasant, at first appearance anyway. I see myself hovering over my body asleep, or am I dead? Then I look at the top of my head and a rat has burrowed through it and is eating my brain.
Yuck Horrible!

However I realise symbolically that it is the death of the mind. Next, I hear a song being sung faintly in the background but I cannot quite catch the words. My body is twitching now and I can feel the waves of energy flowing up and down. Someone is thinking of me and I can feel it swirling around in my sacral; just as I did, prior to your calls to say Goodnight. Then I hear your voice loud and clear, as it has been said to me so many times before, "Keep the faith sister." The song suddenly bursts forth and now I can hear the words.

You've got to have faith… faith… faith.
Now I am laughing at the memory of your face.

In your sudden realisation, as you had voiced out loud. "OMG - Your next book… I am in it!"

"Keep the faith brother." As in your words "over and out."

My gratitude to DAY 1

Good night and God Bless. May the Goodness of the day stay with you? For the Universe is a friend.

Always x

DAY 2

Good Morning and God Bless for may the Goodness of the day be with you. As the universe is a friend.
Always.

8:00 - A lay in how wonderful there is nowhere to go, no one to see only me. The word ME jumps out, See thyself… Lol, this will be an interesting day. I had a disturbed night with dreams flashing in and out mainly fearful ones. The body and the mind react to fear on a cellular energy level. So as soon as the noticing occurs, I purify it in the visionary white flame. As it does not serve me, my physical body or my emotional health, to hold onto this feeling for too long as otherwise I am taking it in too far into the body and allowing it to settle within, so I let it go. Fear is also doubt. I am informed so never doubt yourself. A memory pops to mind of my parents saying to me, "You can do anything Tracy, if you put your mind to it."

The very first noticing I had this morning on waking was the position of my body in the bed, it reminded me of Jesus being bound to a stake, for my hands were above my head crossed and my feet crossed at the bottom. I never sleep in this position. I thought how strange. Maybe this 40 days 40 nights is a period of reflection and then a new beginning, another rebirth so to speak as if I've not had enough so far….so much change, especially in these past few years, now how much more can there be? I have learned during this time, not to think too much, just to trust and have faith in something higher than myself who knows what it's doing.

With that thought, a sudden vision flashes before my eyes. I saw you my friend sitting somewhere looking rather serious. Deep in thought like Socrates…Lighten up man, the sun is out and it is a beautiful day. As I look out into nature, there is so much to be grateful for and we are so blessed to live on this gorgeous planet. The wind is blowing the crumpled leaves away ready for spring. The water has washed the earth overnight and given us and the plant kingdom, the much needed water to drink; it has nourished the vegetables for our food and replenished the trees, for without the trees we would not be breathing this air so fresh. We should be honouring the trees, for they take in the Carbon Dioxide and give us life, the Oxygen that we need, for without this we perish... humanity will cease to survive without the trees. The fire element gives us that warmth, the warmth of the sun upon our faces and the flames of which we can cook our food with. We can also purify our thoughts by looking restfully into the golden glow and watching the flames as they dance and change colours through blue to white, throwing in all the thoughts that no longer serve us, the anger, the jealousy, the hatred in our hearts release them into the fire and watch them, as they burn away.

The Earth...Mother Nature just what can I say about you, for nothing will truly explain your beauty. The colours so rich and vibrant, the reds, the greens, the oranges, the yellows, the pinks, the blues, the violets, the whites, so much beauty we are surrounded with, 'An Earth Rainbow of Colour' And as I look to Father Sky, my heart just fills with love for another day alive on this glorious planet. Thank You, Thank You, Thank You, for I am so grateful for this blessed opportunity to live this life on Earth... The Earth element of life.

As I honour the directions North, South, East and West, just as my forefathers did before me, I wonder in which direction the winds of change are blowing today. As I mindfully eat my breakfast, it tastes so delicious; the taste buds are savouring each and every mouthful. My thoughts suddenly jump to my ex-husbands' comment yesterday as he popped by to drop off some provisions of milk, vegetables and chicken. I thank you for I am grateful for your kindness, an aspect of you that I always loved, not only for the food but the four beautiful souls -the children that I was so fortunate to bring into this world. Your comment… "You are mad Tracy, this 40 day and 40night thing, you are mad. It is freezing you know not really the weather for it. All these obstacles you place in the way, I have always wondered why you could not be free, free to enjoy all aspects of life."

I do not react, for I cannot expect you to understand, as we are so different now. My journey has taken me through many stations, most of which you have never seen yet. So how can you feel what I feel, how can you see it if you have never experienced it, for it is impossible to see what is invisible to you? No one can know the taste of fruit, the sweetness unless they have eaten it, how can they?

So I bless you, I bless you so much, for the thirty years, for the friendship, for the learning for it has served me so well and if I am allowed to give you anything, I wish you health, happiness, peace in your heart and above all love, love for yourself and unconditional love for others. Abundance in all things… Bless You, Always.

10:00 - As I try and practice, my thoughts are now hopping back and forth like a naughty rabbit, lol… as beautiful as rabbits are, please stay still. I have lit a candle to focus upon and as I try and merge with the light for a 3-minute meditation at least, I just cannot for today, 3 minutes seems like an eternity. Usually, I can sit for at least an hour as time disappears now but today no… it appears impossible.

Realisation

It's that mind... the fear has entered my energy field, I have allowed it in overnight, so I need some tools to cultivate my inner garden and remove these weeds. As my hand reaches into my Mary Poppins bag, it clasps something, and I quickly pull it out...I see what it is with the feeling of the delight of a child unwrapping a new present. Hurrah that will do, for it is the special 7 chakra rainbow pyramid that my eldest daughter bought me for Xmas that will do the trick.

MESSAGE

Balance - Balance in all things. Regroup and rebalance all is okay. As I think about this gift from my daughter tears well up, as I realise she sees me, she knows me. Thank You, Alice; I love you too so much, for this crystal is now used not only for when I need assistance but for the benefit of all in my Reiki Healing sessions. Copper and Silver apparently are excellent conductors of energy, so I stand this crystal inside a copper and silver hoop, which is placed under the therapy bed. The Reiki energy can then be transmuted into the auras, the energy fields of others, for the benefit of their self-healing process. Thank You, Thank You, Thank You. I am so grateful. Using the crystal, I am now feeling the scattered energy being brought back to the centre, to peace and tranquility, back to the "OM" - The sound vibration as chanted by Buddhists monks and as heard by NASA when they went into space. The sound of the Universe...

A song from my mother's LP collection suddenly bursts through into my awareness, as I remember playing this over and over again as a child. I loved it and would dance around the room.

MESSAGE

Happy, Happy, Happy, Happy talk. Talk about things we like to do. If we do not have a dream, how can we have dreams come true? Thank you as I continue on my chosen path, focus upon my dreams, and remain in positive energy. All is well in the world. As within - As without Today is a TLC day, I can feel it vibrating so deep within my body. Nourish, Rest, and Reside in love Study. It feels like I am being prepared for something... Money suddenly shoots into my awareness as I am looking for another highlighter for my book, as I am forever losing them.

MESSAGE

This planet revolves around money; much-needed love and compassion are still needed. You can have money as it is just an energy which you need to buy your things on earth, abundance in all things... but remember it belongs to the trees and the earth elements, so it stays where it has been found on earth for you cannot bring it home. As I sit so relaxed in front of the fire just staring into the flames, another thought fleets through. "I love you, Tracy, I really do" as I'm listening to the crackling of the wood.

MESSAGE

Do not forget the children... A book opens your hands' story time and turns the pages. Read them your stories, Norman the weary elf, The Magic Kingdom, The Mermaids Journey. Just as you did with Clio when she was small... they were some of the best times spent together. Also, do you remember the stories you used to write for hours, when at your Nan's for the weekend? The Pebble? All healing for children...

12:00 - The fire... I am so peaceful now as I allow the waves of love that ripple through my body to resonate... through the heart chakra, the colour of green, the colour of nature, as it washes all over me and through every cell of my very being.

In my mind's eye, I can see two triangles connected, one above and one below, it is in perfect symmetry. The feeling of alignment within... of the ONE energy.

The Alpha & The Omega
The Male & The Female
The Yin & The Yang
The Light & The Dark

Balanced merged as one. For as within as without. So, you see it can never be an unequal relationship for neither is the lesser one, for those that understand... it is always balance. Always the student and always the teacher. It is the law of the universe. The Lover and the Beloved always... I just pulled three cards for today from the POWER OF LOVE pack by James Van Praagh. How funny they are...

UNITY.
You understand that the love shared with another is amplified and has a ripple effect across the universe.

PURPOSE.
You possess the determination and dedication to consciously demonstrate love.

COMPASSION.
You demonstrate the language of the heart by actively sharing and living love.
Thank You, I believe in love and the truth.

2:20 - The feeling of exhaustion suddenly sweeps over me and I need to lie down, the combination of a disturbed night, energy shifts and a lack of Thyroxin for my underactive thyroid as I forgot to take it... so I sleep for an hour, then suddenly a feeling arises... this old chestnut again... Guilt, I am shaking my head. Know Thyself Well. I am feeling guilty for taking care of my own needs - crumbs self-love, most important. Guilt that I do not have to rush around in the world, 9 - 5 or overnight shifts for I have chosen a different path. No more guilt. STOP it... you are going in the white visionary flame. Goodbye.

Love you, Tracy, as I look in the mirror and reinforce this to myself... Love You.

My work is heartfelt and probably harder in some ways that others dare to tread but do I must and do I will, for there is no other path for me now. For nothing makes me happier than helping others from my place of authenticity. This may be the road less travelled and it certainly is not for the faint-hearted, but if you have courage and love in your heart then there are endless possibilities that will eventually open up for you like magic!

MESSAGE.
You cannot help to heal those who do not want to heal themselves... Similar to what Swami said, "People will come along in your creativity, offend no one, keep an open heart and compassion but do not waste time with those who speak of healing themselves. But do not change within for they are on repeat. For you can lead a horse to water but you cannot make it drink... The dizziness returns and I realise that my handwriting has changed; my eyesight appears a little misty. Another shift? Same pen, same hand, yet different - another occurrence? Study Time.

5:30 - As I sit outside, my awareness comes back to a situation that I have been struggling with. What would Jesus, Buddha and St Francis do?

Forgive… I have forgiven both myself and them for anything that we did not know. Love…I do love them. I always have and I always will love them unconditionally. Then the prayer from St Francis comes to mind. Ahh, Acceptance… Accept the things you cannot change, for you are not responsible for another and their actions. I drew the line at certain behaviour…the boundary in the sand went down, for now at least.

Jesus forgives us all our sins but should we act intentionally to hurt others, I dread to think of how we will all feel because the Akashic records hold every thought word and deed for us to study on our return and then we have to find a way to forgive ourselves. I shudder at the thought. As I study in more depth the lives of Jesus, Buddha and St Francis alongside the Eastern Philosophies. I am convinced more and more that all roads lead to home through the divinity of God's Love, as somehow this appears significant.

The message of, I am the way the truth and the light have always resonated with me, for to reach the kingdom of heaven we have to pass through the heart, the gate of Christ. This is what it feels like to me and I know how so many times, I have been saved in my life, through my own experiences…So I choose to love God, for to me there is only one Love. At the age of 18, synchronicity occurred as I had decided with my younger sister to be christened and confirmed in the C of E church where we lived in Coventry.

It just so happened that a bishop was passing through and held the ceremony. His name was Bishop John Daly, who I later came to find out became a well known missionary. How funny I thought, as I became a social worker for 17 years, until I stepped into my authentic self and changed to an Author Spiritual Teacher and Healer. I would not say I am religious, although I speak of God; it is with the feeling and the depth of God's Love in my heart that I resonate. As I am a spiritual person and embrace all… from all faiths and philosophies, for if they have open hearts full of love and goodness, they are another representation of God. God in goodness and kindness.

Always in balance and never the extreme for any tradition I feel. All of humanity needs love, compassion and kindness… for kindness is magical. The common threads are woven amongst all knowledge and all teachings from nature through to the Christ Consciousness. A rich tapestry of life within us all and reflected in all the scriptures and for that I have a deep respect, for we are all as one. Born from the goodness and we will return to the goodness, from the same place of love. My journey thus far has been full of love, rich in experience and enlightening to say the least, so for that, I am truly grateful.

There have been many golden nuggets along the way which eventually merge as one into liquid gold, which runs through the veins, the heart and the consciousness for those who are willing to do the work and dig deeper and deeper. Mistakes? Goodness, I have made many, so many lessons along the way, so many potholes and experiences but I would not change a thing, not now, for I have started to uncover the truth and see the diamond light within. Know Thyself Well they said over and over again…Am I there yet, I laugh as I repeat this to God at night in my prayers, like I used to say to my father when we were going on holiday to a special place. Are we there yet!!! Self Mastery over oneself is very rewarding... Know Thyself Well.

Funny how things can change so suddenly in a moment's notice, when we fully trust and surrender to something higher than just us, when we have total faith and follow the instructions step by step it is amazing, for the higher self will never steer you in the wrong direction. It is like the steps appear in front of you, all we have to do is follow them Lol... this sounds easy, doesn't it. KISS - Keep it, simple sweetheart...

Years ago, I was gifted the book, 'The Celestine Prophecy' by James Redfield and as I tried to read it...I could not, for it did not appear to make any sense what so ever. It was like reading gobbledygook...so I gave up and placed it away on a bookshelf, collecting dust. About a year passed and I was dusting when that book appeared to JUMP off the shelf at me, so I picked it up and began to read. This time I devoured it word by word, like a sponge soaking up water as if it had a great thirst... It amazed me, thrilled me, I loved it, for then I was ready for its teachings and for what it had to share with me.

Books have appeared in my life over the years through synchronicity and once I had lost a book by Neale Donald Walsh. It was called 'Conversations with God.' During an event where I was working, I decided to look around during the lunch break and came across a charity bookstall. As I leaned on the books with the weight of my hands, I scoured the hundreds that she had with dismay and thought I would never find anything here. When the lady came over, I asked her if she had it and she said she would not know, for it would be like looking for a needle in a haystack, so my heart sank...

With that I looked down and there to my sheer joy was the book I was holding onto with the weight of my left hand. Thank You God, I said…miracles can happen; you just have to believe in them. Thank you Universe, for I am so grateful.

6:15 - Need to eat the body speaks.

Today…I keep getting the feeling the sense that someone is watching me, not a bad feeling just a presence of love and support. I feel into the energy, It is a male, but not my son or my father as I know their energies… who is it then I wonder and as I go to move to walk away, the feeling is they are walking with me. They have stepped back a little as if they have realised I have noticed them. Now I get the feeling that they are not passed over but that it is someone's higher self who has come to visit me to see if I am okay. A friend perhaps but they are not as I remember them. They are stronger now and much more balanced, that's good. I acknowledge your growth too and I am proud of you always, always proud. I am not 100 percent sure which friend it is as both your energies are very similar, as you both have a gentleness and loving energy but I thank you for passing by.

In my leaving, if I hurt you in any way, then please accept my apologies for it was not meant, it was a very hard decision for me as I did not want to leave.

But, I could see many things that were occurring around you both, of which I did not want to witness. Maybe I took the coward's way out, I don't know but I loved you dearly and always will, for I am a true friend always. Also, I had to know that I could be independent of you and not rely upon anyone else at first, for my work, my authenticity needed to come through, as I discovered who I am truly in love. Every day for years now, on and off I have cried…real tears, of love and compassion for the whole situation, and the separation's but in the learning I shall be forever grateful…for both your presences has helped to shape me, into my authentic self and I realise I have been so blessed to have had you in my life. Thank you.

I have never blamed anyone because how could I? In the knowledge that we are all soul signatures, just having a human experience. Once something was said, I will never leave you, and I know you meant it… for I felt what was in your heart and I meant it too… when I said it to you, for there is never any separation not really and my door is always open.

8:30 - Early night, this is the soft cell I feel before the real lessons begin in the wild of the woods. The last few days I have been sheltered by the barn before I leave for 'The Shed'. I've never been quite so alone in the woods before…even with a house nearby, it is going to get very dark… and very still but I suppose I am not alone, really am I? For there is me and my God.

Today has been another lovely day and I am so grateful.

Good Night and God Bless for may the Goodness of the day stay with you. As the universe is a friend.

Always. X

DAY 3

Good Morning and God Bless, for may the Godness of the day be with you as the universe is a friend.
Always.

7:00
A better night's sleep but many dreams from dinosaurs to fathers and birthday parties, awareness of life and how mixed up it all is. The realisation of acceptance plays a part or you have to make a conscious decision as to whom you wish to spend your life with.

The writing has changed again, much neater this time. My awareness grows as to how can anyone treat another in a certain way unless they have experienced it themselves or at least until they have recognised the true meaning of...from within. For conditioning the copying, the cycle of repeat as we are what we know or thought we knew.

MESSAGE
'Know Thyself Well'
ACCEPTANCE will be my prayer for today, for who can truly understand unless they have walked this path. When I think about living life with another, I laugh... for I am sure I would irritate them Lol. Joy is as wonderful as is unconditional love and with the sharing of this feeling...this depth of love within the heart. Surely, I cannot be the only one to have experienced this, as many have found their way before me.

So, I will wait, I will wait and see what and who God blesses me with, as only ONE who truly sees me can be free. Free to be themselves, as they respect me to be mine and after all no bird likes to be kept in a cage... I remember handing this over to God in my prayers some years ago as I made the commitment to follow my path, in the knowledge that my heart is known.

So if I am to be blessed with certain things and someone special along the way, then so be it...for it will be done. I trust and have faith in the Lord. The realisation of my early formative years rushes in as I was so loved, so cared for and so protected, probably wrapped up in cotton wool. Treated with so much kindness from what I remember as being part of a close and loving family. A memory comes back of a prayer I said as a child... Please God if possible, please do not send me back to this place again, for I am so lucky to have been born into this family and I would not want to come to another. Thank you.

So many experiences we shared together, days out, holidays, high teas as a family, good home cooked food, birthdays, Xmas and celebrations of many types with extended family, so much pleasure. Dancing lessons from aged five to nineteen, dance competitions, piano lessons, alongside being told every day I love you. How blessed was I...unbelievable really, I thought all families were the same but how wrong I was, as I grew and saw through the window into others lives. My father always took us into nature and once he taught me how to drink from a stream in South Wales from where he was born in Treorchy... The Rhonddah Valley... 'Always drink from a rushing stream' he said and never a still one, for the water is clear and clean as it falls from the top of the mountain. So many little things...positive ones, but as we grew we realised he had his own issues. God Bless him for he lived in fear... fear of us being harmed or taken away in some way. Overprotective and Judgemental, a strong character he was but he meant well, for his heart did not mean to harm anyone, he was like a frightened child within and he loved his family. His fear led him to become paranoid during his later years but as I look past all that, he was still the same man, full of love I knew as a young child, so I continued to love him with all my heart, for he wanted the best for us all…as he suffered whilst we made our mistakes and learnt our own lessons. What a joy it would be to see him again now, for him to see the changes although I know he can… he was a good teacher and I hope he is as proud of us now as we are of ourselves. Thank You, Thank You, Thank You for without you I would not be who I am. I am so grateful.

All people are products of their early formative years until they grow and begin to question, to peel away the layers of influence that surrounds them from many forms. Not just parents but teachers, friends, work places, etc. etc., all our experiences shape us until we begin to reform and peel away what no longer serves us. As the layers of the onion are peeled away and the issues purified in the visionary white flame, then and only then can you truly know who you are at the core and what you came here to be. Your authentic self. All of the judgments, the anger, the blame, the jealousy, lack etc. all of everything burn it away, let it go, dissolve it in the fire and it will return…on repeat over and over again until one day, it will be no more. It is hard not to be the victim of circumstances especially when it's traumatic but do not let them win, for you deserve the best; otherwise, the world of illusion has taken you hostage, for you have brought into your self-made prison.

SO Break out…and set yourself free to be in LOVE, in its entirety. We all have trauma in one way or another and some are worse than others…for that, I bless you so much, for I would not wish that on anyone but we do not have to become the product of our story.

It is for this reason that I decided to complete some training and become a speaker for the benefit of others, because as my title states. "We are not our story," and through the use of a unique experience… I think people hear its message, for we really are not.

MESSAGE
Humanity is scared to let go off control. As within, As without, As above, As below- allow the flow. Today is a good day…plant the good seeds and watch your internal garden grow. My study of St Francis last night, has me wondering where the original transcripts went, as I can see the goodness that flows through it, not just this but many other transcripts and philosophies. Did man change it in any way though to suit themselves or because they were fearful that men would destroy themselves if they had true abundance in all things, or was it someone else who interpreted it from their own perception? Why would a certain few be chosen, for instance when we all have the capacity to be the student and the teacher? Some do become leaders I know, if it is in their destiny but we can all reach enlightenment if we continue to unravel the truth and know ourselves well, as we are all soul signatures born into human experience to discover our authentic selves and find our way back into the light. For the light can never be extinguished by the darkness. Dig deep and discover what lies beneath your surface, evolve as we are all evolving over many lifetimes of suffering. Celibacy is a peculiar thought because if we were all celibate, then the world would become a self-fulfilling prophecy, as the end of the world would surely happen, as the lineage ran out. Humanity was made for love and partnership as we are social beings but I feel that too many see with their eyes rather than feel with their hearts.

They are drawn to people for the wrong reasons sometimes, so maybe if we were all unable to see the other, we would make choices from Gods Heart of Love and if we were all patient and not afraid to be alone with our own company, then what Gods intended for us would become ours, as the soul seeks to seek itself. This is a beautiful planet, we were born to see its beauty, to awaken like the rose, as it's petals unfurl in the sun, for us to become its beauty as we merge in the oneness of the love. To live in joy and experience the wonders of life in the here and now, in its entirety, as we are whole, we just do not recognise it. As my little granddaughter, only two years old says to me in her wisdom... wake wake Nan Nan wake wake. I love to play this game with her as her chuckles are like sunshine on the brightest of days. Let that love always remain in your heart my darling and do not allow the harshness of the world to take you away, for you are free, free to be yourself. She is blessed to have been born into a loving family with good parents and I pray she stays true to herself, her loving nature, her heart of Grace her greatest gift!

MESSAGE
Kindness Compassion and Love costs nothing for it does not rely on material wealth but solely on what is lying within the heart.

I Am passionate about Love.
I Am passionate about good healthy relationships.
I Am passionate about nature.
I Am passionate about life and this earth for it was created for us to enjoy. In Joy,
I Am passionate about God's Love.
I Am passionate about helping others to discover their inner authenticity.

So, what are we doing... are we destroying ourselves? Or are we making conscious choices to nourish and fulfill our destiny, bringing it all to life, in all its glory? As we each take responsibility for ourselves we can make a difference, for the world would be changed, one person at a time; then the world would become a joyful place. Have you seen a pebble and ever skimmed it across the water...it ripples... it ripples out to a much bigger space...than where it was We can all start with one thing... US and make a difference.

10:20 OMG...I cannot think and its only day 3. The more I merge, the less I BECOME... if that makes sense because the mind is not in control. I've had to look back in my diary to see what day it is today and I am laughing here, as can you imagine day 39. Oh dear, I will pray that God keeps me sane. Staying grounded will help, being in nature is like a dual-edged sword as nature grounds but it also elevates like the seesaw... so balance Tracy balance, in all things as I drop my attention to, my feet as instructed by a good friend and Mindfulness teacher I know. Ground... I'm feeling so excited for today as I am having some contact with the outside world, as my burnt foot needs a new dressing. Just like a child... how can one simple ride to see the nurse on a bus bring me so much pleasure, as it is like I am getting ready to go to a party? Lol. Appreciation of the simple pleasures in life... Lest we not forget.

4:00 My return... well that was totally different from what I had expected, as first of all, I was nearly taken away with my beautiful deer design umbrella in the strong winds!!! We nearly had a real-life Mary Poppins occurrence... Goodness, this weather is crazy, one-minute strong winds, rain, hail and then bright sunshine all in one day? As climate change keeps crossing my mind, I got into the bus, the energy just hit me like a smack on the face... I have been out of the world for nearly three days only and the suffering I can feel, it is like treacle in the energy fields of the people travelling to the village.

Oh dear, is this how it really is now or am I seeing it from a different perspective because I have changed somehow.

As I link into the energy of the people, not one had greeted me with a smile although I was smiling when I got onto the platform, not even the driver. An older man who looks in his eighties watches me with interest, as I think he can feel something, but still he does not smile back. All I can sense is frustration, and sadness, all people isolated from each other, even the mother with her three best-behaved children. Where was the chatter, the smiles and the laughter... where had it all gone? As I look at their serious to grown-up little faces... what state have we allowed ourselves to get into I wonder. As I soon arrive at my destination, I quickly call into my daughter's home so she knows I am okay and I listen with eager ears as she tells me her news. Well done Alice - You are taking baby steps on your journey and I am proud of you, for I knew you could do it as I have believed in you always.

You may all have been raised by the same parents, in the same way but you are all unique, your own authentic selves and I am proud to have brought you into this world, for you are making a difference. It is so lovely now to back in the silence after my return to the barn, the outside world seemed so noisy. A small village, yet it appeared to have the sound of a motorway as the cars whizzed past, one after the other. The difference in just three days is quite startling, as I have been disciplined in my own practice for the best part of three years now... but three days? How could this change be so rapid?

Is it the years of the monthly FM Alexander Technique lessons, added to my self-discipline, of looking within, during twice-daily meditation and self-development? I do not know the answer as I continue to work on my own personal path but one thing I know for sure is, as I feel it in my heart…destiny is calling me.

Once the momentum has started… there is nothing I can do to stop it… I know that but as I look at myself now and the changes within, I could no more step off this pathway, as I could never stop the love, for it has brought me so much joy already. A message I had in Essex from a friend just before leaving the area. I had thought I was coming for a visit up north but obviously, the universe and God had other plans. My friend suddenly said I have just received a message for you. They are saying - Just follow the steps! One by one they will appear… all you have to do is follow them and as I left my room in a shared house, something made me turn back as my intuition told me to pack certain other items. My logic tried to kick in and override my intuition, as I thought to myself but I do not need those things for I am only going for three days. That is what I thought… Lol… as my ego tried to tell me I am right and sabotage me from my path but I know better than not to listen to my intuition… for it will only cause me problems if I do. Five months later, as I am writing this from 'The Shed in the Woods'…never could I have imagined where I would be…Who I would be with… and where I would be going.

Such fun!!!I love that sitcom 'Miranda'. Not that I get to see it much these days as I do not have a TV but that line from her mother always made me chuckle. Such Fun!!! Life can be like a comedy once you allow the flow to grow. I can't believe it! Was the other line I used to love, from Victor Meldrew…Well, I do believe it…now anyway.

Good Night and God Bless for may the Goodness of the day stay with you. As the universe is a friend.
Always. X

DAY 4

Good Morning. May the Godness of the day be with you. The universe is a friend.
Always.

As I awoke, I could immediately feel the rushing sensation within and as I laid and listened, linking into its feeling of motion, as it reminds me of the ocean waves as they cascade and crash gently to the shore. I could lie here with this feeling but today I cannot, for it is a working day. The rain has started to fall, trip-trapping on the skylight of the barn as it makes sweet music in the silence. The bed feels warm and for once I relish this, as I am basking in the feeling and the sounds around me, like I am lying somewhere on a summers' day.

Breathe I say to myself... for I am about to switch on the phone and allow the outside world into my sacred space. On it goes... ping ping ping ping... what sounds so loud now...ping ping ping ping. Messages and emails... 543 of them, how ridiculous! A noticing occurs as the outside world is feeling very intrusive into my world of Peace. However, I am looking forward to this contact with the people, so I allow it to go over my head as I detach from the distraction of the noise. The body is calm and so is the mind at the moment, so it does not have quite the same effect anymore... the same pull has gone, for I can see to it because I choose to but not because I have to.

Everything in life is just a decision... balance in all things good. As I place my awareness of the word BALANCE, my legs feel wobbly... My practice beckons...for it has become a way of life for me, not just now but over these past years and as nourishing and energising as any food or get well medicine. The discipline of the equilibrium…setting you up for the day is very much needed when engaging with the chaos and the busy pace of the outside world. Even if you begin for only 3 minutes a day - Am and Pm. The results can be dramatic, for practice can be done with the eyes open, anywhere and every hour if necessary, through your difficult days. As you bring yourself, your energy back to zero… to centre in the heart of love. As you refocus and regroup yourself, all will become well in the world, in the inner world and then the outside world does not affect you so greatly. I love my inner world, for I have cultivated it and planted good seeds, for it has grown into a little oasis, a paradise, my nirvana.

8:40 - As I emerge from some practice, I am acutely aware of the fact that I have to adhere to worldly time today, as people are on the clock…the man-made clock, as it spins its hands of time. As I finishing my sitting, I feel the swirling sensation of my sacral, the beautiful female goddess of energy, as she weaves her magic and as it spins gently, and a song appears. I finish my practice and then play the song on my phone. It is, 'How Deep is your love by Calvin Harris & Disciples'.

So I dance around with the feeling of the song in my heart, as I sway to the flow of the music.
Breakfast…Tick
Shower…Tick
Tick Tock goes the clock…OUT the door now for work.

Garden Station Langley…Good company plus the bonus of tea and cake, what more can I ask for today… Life Is good, I say. Good not that anyone believes me. A reading completed, someone else for Drum Circle on the last Sunday of every month and I am enjoying all the moments as they unfold.

Commit and it comes forth as they say… or as a friend once said to me too, it is true… you were right, I will give you that one Lol… Reflecting on the day, as I speak to my Shamanic Teachers down south on the phone. The universe seeks to balance itself in the light and the dark, as I had not realised just how much of a difference there would be already, in 4 days of being in silence. So much noticing of suffering… out there in the world, in people in their hearts and minds and how this suffering is unique to each individual and their perception. For what could be extreme suffering to one, could be nothing to another. They would scoff… at such a notion using their mind of judgment.

Life and people are like a rich tapestry interwoven, all unique with their own colours, vibrations and soul signature songs… Amazing really when you see the bigger picture, so what is it that gets in the way. The formed personality? The Mind? for we are all soul signatures, our version of our "Goodness… our God-ness" having a human experience, here on a beautiful planet so why are we not all sharing and caring for each other.
Why do we not live in peace?
Why do we not love each other as ourselves?
Why do we not all bring out the best in each other?
Each individual has a base of knowledge and wisdom, a skill set which they can acquire if they dig deep enough for them, for they are born to find them.

Some are the truth sayers and the way-showers… a sudden thought emerges of some, I have known and I laugh at myself and check in… for am I using my own judgment here? Or did I see through their illusion? For the personality and the ego can get in the way if we are not careful, it can overtake the soul if it becomes too prideful or strong in any way and then we are in trouble. Big doo doo. For judgement and control, especially control can be the undoing of ourselves and unfortunately others around us too, who have allowed themselves to have been sucked in and influenced. As we have not yet learnt fully to listen to our own whisperings of the truth, we can get caught out, as we do not see it coming, as it can creep up behind us. A lesson learnt not a nice one but a lesson learnt all the same and not to be repeated.

The pantomimes of life… Just as my children loved to go to see them… they are behind you!!! I laugh now at the irony of it all, as in life too, so we all need to be careful and are blessed if we are gifted with vision and ability to use our intuition to help us to see through illusion.

MEMORY

I saw a sign once, so I bought it for my youngest daughter and it still hangs on her bedroom door… It said. "Don't grow up, it's a trap" In a way it is, for when we grow up, then you have to dig deep and undo yourself again… Find yourself again. If we all stayed full of wonder like a child, appreciative of all the little things and full of unconditional love, would the world not be a wonderful place. The harsher energies of the world have tried their best to eat into me today, so I went for a brisk walk in the woods with my drum and played it loud and clear, to regroup my energy. I am freezing… my body is saying, 'It is March you know! Not summer, you need layers of warmth and gloves, even maybe cardboard. Oh, crumbs… Survival…I am starting to think like a homeless person.

A funny memory of my Nan comes to mind. "Have you got a vest on Tracy? It will be the death of you." You know what Nan…this time for once you could be right… Lol. These March winds doth blow. Brrr. A sudden thought occurs… Would I steal if I felt deeply in survival? Maybe… who knows, so best not to judge, as I too have made mistakes in my own life in various ways.

Justify…would they justify it to themselves if they too have given?

Maybe…best not to judge, for we are not to know the reasons why, and as there heart is known by God anyway, so they will eventually know for themselves, as we all will. Just Love…love anyway regardless and forgive always. Well, I am blessed, for I have warmed up.

I have eaten good home cooked food.

I have drunk tea and been cuddled.

I just LOVE to be cuddled, for I am very tactile…

And I have been cuddled with so much unconditional love by the DOG!

I have been sent good wishes from friends and family alike, with a little contact today, so I am blessed, so blessed and I am very very grateful.

The song suddenly starts up in my brain… The Saints go marching on… Good Lord, I am definitely not one of them, for I have made so many many mistakes… believe me!

Good night and God Bless for the universe is friendly to me. A short one again today, for the world has taken me away…

Always X

DAY 5

Good Morning and may the God-ness of the day be with you. The universe is a friend.
Always.

Gosh, day 5 and I cannot believe how fast it is going already. What a beautiful day it is, as I look out of the window and see the redness of the sun shimmering on top of the Pennine hills... so stunning. The sun is shining, the birds are chirping, the wind is less harsh this morning. Funny how something so small can become so exciting. I am not a fan of the cold, Lol... it is a good day.

Realisation.
As I continue to get 'To Know Thyself Well', I realise I am vain! as I dry my hair as it has to be washed daily to look okay before I venture outside. Today I am working so I must look okay... ha there it is again. Do I really care about what others think of me? What I look like? Perhaps I do!

My training as a hairdresser, as a young woman has stayed with me and the years of having to set the perfect hairstyle for dance competitions... Honestly so vain, Tracy. Yet as I think about a friend who suffers from Parkinson's, how insignificant it is, it feels nothing in comparison with what she faces every day. Maybe I need to shave it off, I think to myself... She has been battling with the return of a GDNF trial, as 4Million is required for another one to take place and as the first two have failed, based on clinical statistics, it is looking unlikely that there will be a third. The stats were not good enough for further funding, so raising the money privately will be the only way they can have hope back again for a cure, as shown on BBC 2. Human Guinea Pigs they were, as they volunteered but as I think about how the results were measured, it seems unfair. They all had brain operations and infusions directly into the brain, but the ongoing scans were not included in the stats… which showed my friend had a 63% improvement.

Just look at the videos of the people, as the results to me speak volumes, as I cannot believe it was a placebo effect, as people regained their lives and lost most of their disability, so had it continued who knows what may have happened, maybe a miracle? Science is good but it can sometimes take a lifetime or more to prove and that is too late for some. My son is one of them as he battled with Cystic Fibrosis whilst hundreds of thousands were raised for research, for the ever elusive cure… All that money and scientists are some of the most clever people on earth, so get a move on I have to say as lives are diminishing.

We are people, not sloths so lead the way… Motivated action in love energy… can create miracles I am sure of it. Einstein was sure of it too, as he looked for the impossible and he found it, even though electricity could not be seen, he knew it was there and he believed it until it was so. Today has passed in a bit of a whirl as my journal is filling up fast. When out of silence, further discussions and processing takes place, as I make sense of it all. The Garden Station is beginning to draw people into the magical energy of the place, as it is bubbling… As I look around the grounds, I am back in the world and it is good as here people are smiling, happy chatter rings through the garden, children laughing, lives being lived and stories shared, for the energy here has an uplifting effect on everyone.

Even if just sitting in nature, alongside good food and friendship as friendships begin, for friends are just strangers not yet known. Also, some friends are like kin, as they appear to become like the family that we choose for ourselves… My book launch Numerology card readings, Reiki, drum circle filling up, a talk and a workshop all planned. I love the feeling of the energy as it moves in creativity and expands at its best in Love… and self-healing, for we are so blessed.

As I link into technology as most of the world appears to live there now, I catch up with old and new friends alike, as I go back into silence until next weekend and will soon switch off. I am tired but happy, content as I have been in service today and able to assist others in helping themselves, but I also realise that perhaps the soul needs to be on the net, in its goodness in its god-ness, in its creativeness. Something to ponder… I am so grateful, for today has been another wonderful day.

As I relax for the evening and listen to the fire, I further explore where my life could be heading and as I let go of the mind in thinking the feeling of sinking… further and further within is becoming evident. Each time I return to the stillness, the silence of the within…it drops down to another level, one that has not yet been visited and it is deep… like the ocean… I can feel it as the energy hums away inside me. I did not realise how far away we are from our true selves, our souls calling, and as I link to the core, the best that I can, it amazes me, that still, and it appears like I am only scratching the surface. If we could all tap into our resources, our true gifts in all their fullness, I bet we could do so much, as I surely believe that we barely use 10% of our true capacity. Hidden corners and sections of the soul to be accessed at any time, what a discovery that would be like a gold mine. I wonder how long it would take to reach this goal… No need to give up Tracy, as coupled with science and technology, who knows what's around the corner, it could be amazing! I stop for a moment and view my body in the chair in my awareness…just sitting there… nothing to do. Can I see any muscles switched on, am I holding myself in any way? As I let go of my shoulders and allow my arms to fall relaxed to my side as I breathe out.

The skeleton is holding me, not my brain or my nervous system, so I allow it to fulfill its purpose and let go, surrender as the physical is built for a job, as I don't need to 'do' anything but just be. Old habits die hard. For I suddenly spring up out of the chair without a thought, what for? When I did think of taking that action? As not even a second registered so I could intervene...

as I went on automatic pilot. At least I am aware of it, I think at this moment, as I wait before I move and assess the situation. What do I need to do to walk ahead, swing my arms, no but just bend my knees and allow the body to go, as it has a function? Practice, Tracy Practice for it will serve you... always.

Meditation and as I think about linking into the consciousness, I realise I am in it, for my egoistic mind tries to convince me again that I am on my own but I am not, as the divine thread holds me like a puppet from the cosmos through to the crown of my head and down......through to my heart, the heart of grace. I am always linked in...for I am never separate from the oneness of the universe, for it is like a dot to dot... a matrix and we are always aligned.

As within, as without, as above, as below allow the flow. Do not forget Tracy and let ego cut you off in the illusion, stay connected in the awareness that you are one. This reminds me of the poem that I wrote last year during 2018. The elusive, as that is how it seemed, one minute it is with you and then it is gone as it disappears. You have it in your grasp, you understand it, you feel it, and then no... it goes until later on it stays a little longer and then longer, as you get to know yourself well. I shall share the poem here, for it is wonderful once felt and registered within one's heart.

THE ELUSIVE.
Where art thou now?
In this moment…
I can feel you in my heart…
Silence… my heart listens for it can hear…
I can see you in my mind, & in the reflection of a pool.

You are as pure and as clear as the air
A sudden breeze that caresses my face and whispers through the leaves.

You are in the sky, the stars and the sun
In every molecule of my very being, in essence, you and I are one whole…yet where…
No beginning and no end…a nothingness of space and time continuum… a peace…
A deep, deep peace that can be heard like a hum….

Om Shanti… Om Shanti…Pray…hear me speak… let go of all that you believe you are… and be…be in the mini second, the heartbeat, the trees, space… the beauty and the joy.

Be in all things… as we live… For we are alive… awake… vibrating…more alive than ever before… for we are as ONE with the universe.

It still amazes me what can suddenly come out of what appears to be nowhere, when we take the time to listen to our soulful selves… within. Discipline Tracy, always discipline…for it has served you well thus far and will continue to support you in love and grace, for you are never alone. I decide to switch off now as the silence is calling me, how I wish I could record it for you all, as it almost sounds deafening, and it is bliss…

Good night and God Bless, may the God-ness of the day stay with you. The universe is a friend.

Always X

DAY 6

Good Morning and may the God-ness of the day be with you. The universe is a friend.
Always

6:30 - I wake up to the feeling of the swirling energy within as I lie resting and listening to the universe within but then a sharp interruption as the body speaks, where is that loo? Quick... I am not in Noah's ark but there could be a flood, so like a dancer doing the quickstep I rise out of the bed and shimmy across the floor. My last few hours here before I enter the shed, fully enter and leave the shelter of this sanctuary. My transition into the shed is now over as this becomes real now, so I eat my breakfast in the garden for the last time at least for the next seven weeks, as I watch the sunrise and listen to the birds. I wish now that I had taken up lessons in the identification of bird song, as there is such a variety of songs being sung. Such beauty of the bird kingdom alone...

REALISATION.
It's a comparison to languages and cultures, as we are such a rich earth in every way. Noticing, as I write in my journal, I notice that my writing is now leaning to the left, is this the left brain in its creativity, I wonder? As I look through the previous entries, my writing has changed from left to right and in style too, sometimes italic, or scripture, some with controlled lettering, others open swoops of the pen and some neat... it is strange how much it continues to alter and sometimes I struggle to spell or read my own writing.
The more I go into silence, the more things change...

54

My final meditation and then I will be leaving here... I am wondering now on my return... will I be the same or different?

Will I have any hair? Oh dear, I am laughing now at the thought of it as the pull to have it shaved appears to keep coming back to the surface. Life is funny at times but so enjoyable...

MEMORY

At a laughter Yoga class I was holding in Essex, I was speaking about the various tools that I have used myself for my own self-development and the years of FM Alexander Technique lessons. As I continued to explain, the whole group suddenly began to perform with a sitting to standing lesson following my verbal instructions... hilarious I thought and laughed as I said, 'Wrong teacher wrong group', as we were all laughing at the natural occurrence. Shifts in awareness were both a pleasure and a menace... as I voice out loud, 'Where is that cup of tea?' I am sure I just made it, as I have lost something else... Symbolic for sure.

When following this work, as you undo yourself you can become lost in a sense sometimes even within your own house, lost in an apartment, in your own head or even your own life for a while as things dismantle and then rebuild onto a stronger foundation.

I have just caught myself talking to myself... lol... it's silent, so no one else to talk. As that flashes up a memory of a time with a friend as they saying their noticing...

'You are talking to yourself... Tracy as I reply with a little white lie... no I am not. I am talking to you Lol and anyway Pot kettle black! As you do it too.'

Shift Shift... how many stations are we through now. All the goodness flows from the centre from the heart of grace and pure love, I am feeling very fluid today as I am walking faster with a glide... and much more energy inside.

OBSERVATION.

I am observing the glide of the mop over the kitchen floor... with ease as it goes from left to right no pushing and pulling, just flowing as the movement in action occurs, the ease of motion. The allowing as it just works, nothing to do but allow the movement to take place with the physical working as it should with ease. As I glance at a photo of me standing at the Garden Station, I can see immediately that I am holding myself in some way, as my arms are slightly away from my body and the muscles immediately let go in recognition as my arms relax and slide down to the sides, hanging as nature intended them to do from the shoulders and supported by the skeleton... nothing to do except be.

MESSAGE

The council of nine and thirteen, the ascended masters and the Godhead, the One energy. There are universes beyond universes through the one and beyond. Science just has to catch up and prove it, so as people open up their hearts and minds it will be seen and known. It is not the fear of God, as God is the goodness of consciousness but is the fear of ourselves as we look within. For what we see and recognize, we can heal and change, so we stop the cycle of repeat, like the hamster wheel.

What a wonderful opportunity we have here on earth, to do it now before we return and look in our files and records of our achievements and fails... Every thought, word and deed was done by ourselves, our intentions and judgements. All the loving things too but now in awareness we can choose which to do so... choose wisely in your wisdom and choose love always. The healers heal. Nature heals.

Science, when used for good, can prove and heal. The magical realms - use your spells for goodness only to heal and create in love. Are we listening, as the earth is a beautiful planet full of riches? The way has been shown and has been for centuries, only if we take the time to stop for a while and listen with an open heart.

Nature really has been at its best today as the colours are all springing forth into bloom with the flowers and the bushes in spring. Rabbits are running back and forth to their burrows and the stream, the rushing sound of the water as it cascades and tumbles over the rocks. This silence is magical, for in its silence you can truly hear all the delights of the world.

As dusk draws near and the darkness starts to fall, I continue to sit outside of the shed listening intently to the "Evensong". So loud and glorious, as the birds all sing in chorus. Suddenly an owl swoops around circling the woods like a night watchman, or a parent as it says goodnight to its children, as all the birds then fall silent… no sound. I continue to sit and listen to the bubbling of the stream nearby and a car's engine as it passes in the distance. I laugh inside and think I hope no one walks near and stumbles across me for they would jump in surprise to see me sitting in a grey dressing gown and slippers with my hood up looking like a very odd monk! I think somehow I would frighten them more than they would me.

Night vision glasses… that's what I need, as I remember my favourite glen in the highlands. As it used to come alive at night with foxes, badgers, owls and deer. I am wondering are they near here? They must be. I have fed the birds and placed out fresh water for their breakfast, so tomorrow I shall sit outside and watch to see if any creep by.

Study time.

As I decide to read through the bible tonight, I am amazed at what I am finding, for before these 40 days had begun, I had a message which said 'speak in tongues'... I did not even know what this meant!

But as I read further, there is a passage which speaks about tongues... oh crumbs. Also the path of St Francis and the countries he visited, as I have already started with Assisi, as directed last year. As you travel to spread the joy and the love through your work, the message said and then as I find Mark 1 Forty days in the wilderness... The prophecy, it startles me... For a sudden memory shoots through my mind from a place, with a friend as a stranger suddenly announces to us both. It is the prophecy. You are hearing it repeated out loud... as hundreds are saying it everywhere we go. Did you hear that Tracy? As they linger... with a smile and a stare. Yes, I said as I quickly walked across the room for a cup of tea, to calm my nerves.

She later takes me to one side and reiterates...This is the start of it for you two, as it is a spiritual partnership for the greater good of all and nothing can be done to stop it. But I cannot control another I say... so now what? As I think to myself, just pray and hand it over to the consciousness in the hope that one day, they too will hear the calling. As I gaze at the earth, it appears to be heaving... as if it's breathing so I go inside and lie down. Now the energy is building like waves as they are growing in strength and rushing through my internal universe, flowing fast, up and down my chakras as I suddenly feel dizzy... another shift? Significant I feel.

7:30 - I go back outside... just pitch blackness, no lights, no sound, no nothing, just darkness... Yet somehow I do not feel afraid, for I am not really alone, I am not separate, I am whole. As my eyes begin to adjust, I suddenly hear the owl again as he probably sees me clearly. The thought of the Garden Station fleets in, as 3 years ago I popped in for a cup of tea, now look at me. A year later I was invited to an event with my little red wigwam, where I held positive empowering readings. Now, look...as another transformation has occurred, and The Inner Guru Propagator returns, to help people weed their own inner selves and plant the good seeds.

Confused? Don't be for I am here to assist you in healing yourselves and discovering who you truly are at core... For you to find your golden nuggets, your inner wisdom and your gifts that you have to share with the world. Your authentic self, so that you too can live in joy and with love. An early night for me tonight, as I am hoping to wake up with the Dawn Chorus!

Good night and God Bless may the God-ness of the day stay with you. The universe is a friend

Always X.

DAY 7

Good Morning God Bless and may the God-ness of the day be with you. The universe is a friend.

I missed it! Can you believe it? I missed the Dawn Chorus as I slept like a log within the shed. Dreams... dreams that I remember however invaded my space as there were many throughout the night. The birds are happy as I sit outside with my cup of hot tea, listening to the sounds of nature in the early hours. A baby robin decides to join me, then a rabbit runs by surprised to see me, the sight of such a thing invading his world, his space here in the wood. As I listen, I can hear a loud tapping, very loud on wood... 'do we have woodpeckers?' I think to myself. No, where to go, nothing to do when in a flash the emotion of guilt rears its head, it is here again as it rushes up out of nowhere. Feeling guilty as I am not rushing around with children, work or anything. But I cannot be responsible for the world, I have done more than my fair share, so this is my time, for me to go within and see what secrets lie there. The world suffering is not mine, although I will do what I can anytime but I can only start with me and change within as I start to see what I need to do.

So I release it with love, for we are all on our own journey, each of us treading on our own unique path and it is our responsibility as an individual to discover just that. Bless us all, as easy it is not but as things start to appear, it becomes clear and then we are near to the spot. The part where we start new and afresh in a good way, stable as we set down the foundation of the planting of the good seeds... As I try to think, I realise it becomes harder for if I could make a decision today, it would be good for the mind escapes me in every way. The Shaman's Oracle by Matthews and Will Kingdom appears to beckon me, so I pull myself some cards.

Hunter of abundance.
Ancestor of hope.
Ancestor of illusion.
Spirit of truth.
Shaman of tradition.
Dancer of life.
Dancer of reconciliation.
Shaman of reflection.
Shaman of sorrows.
Hunter of death/ancestor of skill.
Dancer of Joy and dancer of beginnings.
Transformation it is then!

So I take my rattle and honour the directions, along with Father Sky and Mother Earth while giving thanks for all the support, the care and the love that surrounds me in my life, for I am truly blessed. Thank you for I am so grateful.

As I go to wash, I shiver with the cold as a strip wash in the cold. Water is supposed to be good for you. Lol... then I remember a pan and fill it with water and heat it up to wash my hair... it feels glorious as I laugh to myself and think yes, Tracy, you are an idiot. A memory of a boyfriend at just 18 years of age as his words ring in my head. 'We could never go to India' he said, you would never manage without your hairdryer... 'Know Thyself well.' Wonder what he would say now if he could see me in the shed! Maybe my hair should come off or at the very least be cut short - very short for then I could just wash it and leave it...

A thought occurs… I am grey underneath… all these years of a nice and easy hair colour, at 56 years young and beautiful inside and out but as I look in the mirror, I think to myself 'What would I look like, a man? Or a monk?'

Here it is again vanity… Who cares. Do I? I have had to think further on that one. But as I look again, I remember my friend with 'Parkinsons'. For Goodness sake Tracy, it is only hair and it grows as the feeling comes again, off off off with the hair…can I do it? Will I do it? Who yet knows!

Breakfast in nature, as I sit outside watching the birds with delight, as they have found the seeds that I put out on their tables. The robins, the chaffinches, all busy flitting to and from the tables, watching me as I am watching them, as we both eat our plenty, for we are so blessed.

10:00 - Meditation in the wood. A memory springs to mind of a place where I first lived alone after my father's death and my separation from my husband. I lived in a small village, surrounded by a wood and it was beautiful as I loved to walk past the totem poles down by the stream and deeper within the forest trail where I would sit and meditate in a special spot I had found.

MESSAGE

Go to the stream and kneel down, take some water and place it on your head as we want to bless you… That is weird I thought but as I have learnt to listen to my higher self, the intuition and not the ego I followed instruction. Then as I go to leave, I make a decision to go home a different way and I followed a path which led out onto the main road. A change I thought and maybe easier than going back the same way. But then as I started to walk, I suddenly heard a message shoot into my mind. Run…Run, turn back and go into the wood. My heart starts to pound and I almost ignore it as my ego and logic tries to intervene with…don't be silly; there is nothing wrong. But then it comes again, this time with a real urgency…

Run. Turn back and go into the wood and hide. With that I run, I run as fast as I can with the realisation that I need to be fitter as I am tiring breathless, as I pass through the trees I hear again Hide, Hide now.

Before me is a large oak tree, so I quickly hide behind its trunk, although I can still see the road, I cannot see anything. Then in the distance, I begin to hear a faint sound, of an engine as it draws closer and closer. My heart is now beating so loud as I hold my breath. I fear it may stop. I can now see a quad with a man upon it, he stops for a second as if surveying the land. Please God, I say make me invisible for I am not sure I am in deep enough. Stay still the inner voice says and with that, I lose my footing and a twig cracks… The man looks and I freeze behind the tree, for what feels like a lifetime maybe only a minute but I dare not look or move as I am frozen to the spot.

I can no longer see him but can he see me? Soon, I hear the engine as he revs it up and starts to move away. My legs are like jelly but as he starts to leave, the inner voice shouts again NOW! Run deeper back into the forest and follow the path home. This time I do not question not for a second as I really run… and reach the place I call home my new house. As I sit with a cup of hot tea, I reflect on my experience, for not everyone is good at heart as they have chosen to use their free will in the wrong way and they are very misguided. We are all born from goodness onto this beautiful planet but we all have the double-edged sword. The gift and the curse of free will…

Some will discover the truth and some will not will I...I hope so. The mirror on the wall stands before me. What do you see Tracy... What beauty lies within thee.

10:30 - Time for hot water with lemon and Italian honey, purchased when in Italy and a pinch of mixed spice. Then a walk. Reflection - Nourish. My hands are cold but my heart is warm. It is March and homeless people need gloves, I am not homeless for I am in the shed and its luxury. Meditation - Chants of Om and Ra for peace and dissolving illusion. What can I do? Pray, speak, change within and love, for as you love they love too.

Emotion.
I hate to see others suffering and to feel their pain but I can only save myself and take responsibility for me, as I know the answer before it is received...

Surrender...
Sit in a place of trust faith and with love in your heart, as I place my hands together in prayer. Help me God, Help me...

I place a drop of the holy water I have collected from my retreat in Assisi on my forehead and I decide to go for a walk in nature.

12:30 - As I reach a spot to sit and have a picnic lunch, a robin comes to watch me eat, so I place a few crusts on his table for sharing as my thoughts drift back to my retreat in Assisi in September. Such a special place and the family I found after listening to my intuition and taking a risk. I had just returned from Croatia after a period of self-development when I felt an overwhelming feeling at the airport to fly back out to Italy. How can I do that I thought but I decided to listen to my heart and ignore my logic as I went home and repacked. As I ordered two tickets, one for me and one for my daughter, as I surprised her too with an impromptu visit as we then flew out together to have an adventure. I rang my friend and informed them that I could no more stay in England another second but that I would see them…later. I had always wanted to see Pompeii since my childhood, as programmes about its history had fascinated me, so off we went to Rome, then Pompeii as I followed my heart and instructions. For there was something, I would find I was told… something that I would learn and that it would be okay.

Clio loved it as much as I did but as I looked at the mummified figures, I cried as I cried for the families who perished and the lives lost so suddenly. I sent healing to the area and blessings for them all, and I shall never forget it ever.

Rome - the homeless, much like London sleeping amongst its great beauty and wealth, it so reminded me of home and its inequality in this rich world. Then we boarded a train and travelled to Assisi, this is where I instantly felt at home, the magical city so blessed by the presence of St Francis. The complex, I found of self-catering apartments just amazing as it is set amongst the hills just a few miles outside of Assisi and the family who owned it was so loving. As they drove us to shops and into the city, Perugia too and made us so welcome.

One morning as I sat by the pool to meditate, I suddenly saw a nun in my mind's eye and she was standing with her back to me but as she turned around and faced me, I was overcome with emotion. For it was a recognition of a friend whom I had shared a life with. The love was immense as she took my arm pulling me in so close in love and hugging me. It is time she said, for you to tread your path, return to this place and bring others to a pilgrimage to St Francis. Follow the ways and the places he visited, hold your talks, your work, for it will spread the joy and open the hearts of people. I will help to guide you she said as you return bringing more people with you and as she left as suddenly as she has appeared I knew, I knew then in my heart that I had to fulfill my calling and my destiny. I booked the venue for the following year and as we departed from this place, I knew something so very special had occurred.

The following year, I did return much to the delight of the family and my first retreat was born. My sister shared in it too and helped with the workshops as she too is beginning to follow her path and it was lovely to be together as sisters... I cannot even put into words the magic that occurred that week, the experiences that were shared, and the work that was completed on ourselves and the places that we visited. The tomb of St Francis and St Damiano.

The sacred art circles amongst the olive trees where we drummed and the caves of St Francis where we walked, mediated and prayed. As it appeared to take on a life of its own, so special and beautiful week was had by us all, we were truly blessed and all because I listened to my gut instincts and followed the message.

So now each year, I return in September with different people, as we walk our path and journey together, as we go within and learn what gifts and discoveries there are for each of us in love. And now as I sit in the shed and read the writings of St Francis during my 40 days, I know other places will be found as Assisi was just the beginning.

1:30 - My energy dips as I listen to the physical and lie down for an hour as so much change already in such a short space of time. My body is asking for healthier foods, smaller portions and lots of fresh air and water. For the longer I sit in silence within nature, the more I uncover about myself, for only when you are alone, with only nature and the animals, do you realise that you cannot escape yourself. Emotions rise again to the surface as I recognise the need for releasing, the letting go of the old to make way for the new. Courage Tracy, I tell myself Courage for you are loved, so very much. Tears flow and I release them into the pillow as I fall asleep, I trust and have faith that all is well.

2:30 - I emerge and sit back outside in the sun as it shines, so I make a drink and just relax… as I open a parcel of songs from my shamanic teachers, I notice a letter and read. As I read it over, the tears flow again, for I can feel their love, their support for my continued journey and I am blessed, so blessed to know them, such special comments; so I thank you, Chris and Nick, for I am truly grateful to have met you! With the beat of the drum, I sing the songs and give praise to the earth, all the directions. The birds join in from the trees, surprised I feel to see such a celebration. I soon have an audience for I am sure they can understand the words as they flow from Ancient Traditions. My drum circle, the last Sunday of each month here at the Garden Station, what fun we are going to have! I bury an orange candle from my Mesa Alter in the woods as I bless clearing a sacred space, as stones have been built by the local children in the same way as shown in the grounds of the St Francis monastery, so I leave them alone with lots and lots of love.

My new white candle for purification has been powered in meditation and prayer and it is placed on the altar ready for working with the people.

5:00 - Chicken and vegetables… so much gratitude for the food and nearly time for study and another meditation. So much to do and the time is evaporating, as an early night beckons again. Rest and re-energise for tomorrow is another day, still 24 hours.

8:00 - Tired, so tired now as it must be all the fresh air, change in diet and learning... The body speaks to me as it says sleep. Thank you to the universe for such a wonderful day.

Good night and God Bless, may the God-ness of the day stay with you. The universe is a friend.

Always X

DAY 8

Good Morning and may the God-ness of the day be with you. The universe is a friend.
Always.

I have realized that I have been sleeping a lot more than usual, straight through with no interruptions. Apart from one night as I clapped my hands to inform a mouse or some other animal that I am present and not to come in. As I could hear it trying to gnaw its way in through the wood in the corner of the shed, it came by on the first night and now it has returned, trying its best to get through to join me in the warmth.

Dreams were aplenty last night, some of which I remember but one in particular, stands out as I can see some friends and go over to hug them to say hello but they become rigid, static and stand still like a statue. I can feel their energy as it is heavy, depressed almost afraid to look at me, and I do not understand why. However as the thought fleets through, I am then shown a vision of a woman speaking to them about me. The personality of the woman is strong, controlling, as she stands in ego and has issues of her own. Judgements are shared and placed upon others, so I leave, with sadness but an acceptance, for if others are influenced then I can do no more but send them unconditional love. I cannot control others or change their actions, as I can only be responsible for myself, so I step back and allow them to follow their path and their freedom.

As the truth will be shown and they will eventually see what lies within my heart, for I have always wished them nothing but the best and love. This morning I am feeling rather groggy, my head is aching, my teeth hurting and my tongue feels sore. Is it the change in diet I wonder, caffeine withdrawal or the seasons, as the temperature fluctuates so rapidly, one minute warm and the next freezing cold. My body is constantly having to adjust to rapid change each day both physically and emotionally and I am not used to it... so I shall monitor it, I think to myself as I gaze at the little birds flocking to their breakfast, for they lift my heart so much. I love all their colours so bright and beautiful... that statement suddenly reminds me of a day when my youngest was small. The school had taken her to a local church for a Mother's Day celebration, where we all attended and each mother, in turn was presented with a small gift that they had made especially along with a bright yellow daffodil. As the words from the song rang through the church, tears of love filled my eyes for this little girl and for this wonderful planet.

All things are bright and beautiful, all creatures great and small. In the end, as I took her hand as we walked up to the leafy lanes towards our home, I knew then I was blessed with my beautiful children and home... We were living in the large farmhouse at the time but now I am so much richer... as I look around the shed, for material plenty is not real, it is a temporary fix. I like nice things and a nice home too but they are not for keeps, only the memories and love are...

I wander in the woods and sing to my heart's content for there is no one around and the sun has come out... all things bright and beautiful, all creatures great and small, all things wise and wonderful, the lord god made them all.

Birds have always been so very special to me, as have my children, family and friends, as I love them all each in their uniqueness. There is nothing like the feeling of holding a newborn baby seconds old, as it rests upon your chest and blinks as it looks into your eyes, the energy, and the connection so beautiful. I have also been blessed twice now in my life to hold the little wild birds… as they have landed on my palms and allowed me to feed them. They have trusted me not to hurt them, while I held them gently and I have never forgotten the feeling, their beauty and their energy.

Once this occurred in a glen in the highlands of Scotland, not long after my son had passed and another time here in Kielder Northumberland, such memories that fill my heart with the feeling of a song.

MESSAGE

Sketch pad and crayons are needed to draw the flowers… Do you remember Bluebell Woods in Coventry where you walked as a child with your parents and sister? As you ran through the woods with the appreciation of nature, as you loved the colour of the bluebells.

I remember it well I think to myself and I have reproduced so much with my own children, as we have appreciated many many areas over the years. Just a few weeks before my son's passing, I stayed in the hospital with him overnight and I cried, as we spoke together and I said to him, I feel I have not done enough! But mum he said you have, you have always done so much. For you took us everywhere… and showed us so many places… picnics, experiences, so much fun was had by us all. Loch Ness, Glen Affric, Stratford upon Avon, The lake district, Ben Nevis, John O Groats, Peddars way, Memorial park, Coombe Abbey, Kenilworth Park, Waxham, Thetford forest, all over the coastlands and so much more…mum you could not have done any more, for you love us all so much and I love you too, remember that always.

Look after my brother and my sisters, keep your dreams mum. I have been saving and I am leaving you £600 to have a little holiday after I am gone, be together as a family and be happy, live again, as I want you to all do well. How blessed was I to have been his mother, so much wisdom he showed in his 16 years... So many years have passed. Yet as I think now how lucky I am, that my path has crossed again with the garden station, a sudden vision appears of the new meditation group as it flashes before me. The round circle with the stone seed in the centre, lights all around and the people smiling with open, relaxed, happy faces.

For when like minds join together from the heart, things grow, magically, organically and turn out to be far better than what we could have planned for ourselves. The canopy is up with faith, alights aglow, the labyrinth is on its way and new projects are in seedling for they are being born out of love.

Only goodness grows where truth and love are sown and as I walk through the woods here today, the first day of spring I look around for the signs of the bluebells. I go within today for long periods, as I can feel the changes begin to ring within my very being and I am silent... listening for signs of any action that I may need to take in your name. For I realise my relationship with God is now in place, as I surrender to a higher power, in trust and faith as I know I am loved.

The heart if full... the lover and the beloved are joined together. Time passes quickly today as I notice that the darkness is beginning to fall, the owl is hooting and I am happy, very happy. I continue to chant. I am healthy as my physical is still a bit slow but I shall carry on nourishing myself and learn to get to know myself well. Dinner is eaten and study time completed as I relax now into my little bed, as

I look around with love in my small shed and wonder what dreams lie ahead for me. Today has been a peaceful day... quiet and wonderful as I have wandered and watched the flowers, the animals and allowed the flow to move through my system.

Letting go...letting go... more and more every day... allowing the flow, no plans just trust in love.

Good Night and God Bless for may the God-ness of the day stay with you. The universe is a friend.

Always X

DAY 9

Good Morning and God Bless for may the God-ness of the day be with you. As the universe is a friend.

I heard it! 'The Dawn Chorus' Day 9 and the magical number as they woke me up. The first bird in the stillness and then the choir, the accompaniment, the symphony the music of nature as they all join in one by one. The many rich healing tones of the bird kingdom natures 'Solfeggio' It was just beautiful as I sat outside drinking my first cup of tea with the ripples of the sounds washing all over me, how can it get better than this?

Day 9 I am so excited but then I remember what I am told. It will be a magical day but watch out for everything, look all around you like the owl and listen. As I sit quietly listening to my inner voice, I hear 'keep the curtains closed just for today' So I check the small light from the window to see if it can be seen and I draw them even closer. During the night, I kept waking a little as fear was rising up from the root chakra to the tip of my crown and it kept coming over me like waves. I am not frightened here for this has become my little home, my Ashram and I feel into it to see if I can pinpoint what the problem is. It is the thought of something that appears much bigger than me, as it feels like a weight of responsibility but I know I am not responsible for any other, for they have to take responsibility for themselves… Am I capable comes to mind, am I up to this job just as the thought had fleeted through my mind when I discovered I was pregnant with my first child? But as I breathe calmly and listen, I hear again, 'You would not be given anything that you cannot handle, so just trust and keep the faith.'

As I go inside and look in the mirror, the pull to have my hair shaved off appears again, it is getting stronger and as I dress and place my shawl around my shoulders and my looped green scarf a gift from a friend over my head. I realise that my whole appearance has changed. I look like someone who has studied for years, or that I have been born to the middle east... but, it is the look of PEACE and LOVE that I can truly see, the soul reflection of my heart in the mirror through my eyes. Emotion comes forth as I realise I have travelled a long way, the hard way sometimes but now I am genuinely on the path of peace. Some may question and that is okay, for you should never follow blindly...questions are healthy, all I say is to stay in Peace and Love always and find your authenticity.

Some years ago, as I searched for a philosophy that I could join I could not find one that truly represented my feelings, some came very close and others were too far away... the extreme but yet I knew we were all still connected. Yet other matters like Astrology and the study of the universe were dismissed how can they be when we are all part of the 'ONE' creation. I have often thought about starting my own philosophy... for then it would represent us all in LOVE so maybe I will, as I can see the connectedness of everything. Nothing is to be dismissed because GOD created it all in its BEAUTY... no man, woman or child should hurt another..this is the primary law and SURELY IN OUR HEARTS WE KNOW THIS.

It is difficult I know, for the curse of Free will still reign for many but as we grow and discover the truth..one day this will be seen, as mans controlled world crumbles with greed and ego, as they cannot share and see abundance for all... however it will be seen one day and PEACE will reign again... for Kindness is magical. Question yes, for sure, as that is healthy, God knows what lies deep within my heart, the same as all of us, as all is known. Become a seeker of TRUTH and leave the illusion. I am losing track of time and day and this no longer appears significant as I am not living to the rules of the man-made world at present, the rush of life is no longer real for me and as I share my breakfast with the birds, I watch them all as they eat their fill. The pheasant, the chaffinch, the blackbird, the pigeon, the robin and now a rabbit, for the rabbit hides behind me. Do not worry little rabbit for I am not here to harm you.

A reminder though to always look around you, for the world has not yet changed to the way it should be… so keep aware of all your surroundings… intuition. A friend has quickly popped by to lend me her dog whilst she goes to work and as we walk together through the woods, I sing and rejoice at the sun as it comes out and beams down upon us. All things bright and beautiful… all creatures great and small. All things wise and elegant, the Lord God made them all. I can see why the homeless sometimes travel with a dog, a faithful friend of unconditional love. I am a seeker of truth I know that as I can feel it in my heart, for God's Peace is glorious.

I Love the Sufi wisdom as it lies within the heart, a place I sit… And as I hold my talks with tales and poetry, I love the mystic and the mysterious way, as I am blessed to know to listen to my own intuition and with the understanding of God's love as I too choose to live and work in the world. 'Know Thyself Well' I Love the Lao Tao as it is a wisdom based on nature just as the ancient wisdom of Shamanic practice shows another of my loves as I am due to qualify as a shaman very soon. Our forefathers lead the way as they were also the nature connectors, the intuitive and the way showers, the truth bearers…for they are all here, their presence remains on the planet for us all to source.

I Love Zen Buddhism for its Humor. All aspects of Buddhism...
.and of course the Dalai Lama. All experienced in the practice of the
here and now, the love and the compassion, for they see the
suffering. The concepts of which I too embrace with love and
respect to all in our connectedness. And of course the 'Awakening',
the gentle awakening like the flowering of the bud, as we open
ourselves up on our own individual journey towards enlightenment.

I Love Sai Baba and how this links to God through the thread, of
which I was shown myself in meditation. I did not know of Say
Baba and one morning I was shown a vision, a vision of him
standing there with his hair...all wide and lovely from his head. I did
not know this man, so I was pulled into looking for him, as they said
I was to go within... in silence... and then as they told me where to
look. His love and his trust in God of abundance, in respect of
everything good in the world, so it resonated with me.

I rang up a good friend to tell them, to which he later says, for what
you did not know was, I know of him and I was looking at his photo
in a shop at the time you rang and discussing him, Ha Ha... how the
Lord works... in mysterious ways. I Love Ganesh and his love of
abundance for all.

I Love Mohammed as he speaks of the 'ONE' God.

I love Jesus and of course St Francis for all have the threads of
Goodness running through them... The healers and the 'Divinity'
The Holy Spirit I love them all, for as their threads interweave
amongst the people, just like the roots of all the trees over the land.
As Above, As below reflected...like in the water and the Tree of
Life. We can join together in GOODNESS. The God-Ness of
'ONE'. The Godhead from whence we came and where we shall

return in LOVE once we have fulfilled our obligations to ourselves, for I feel we cannot enter through the 'gateway' unless we feel Christ within our heart in love, for we need to come through him.

9:00 - I have just been told a man is walking in the woods with an open rifle so I will pray this is the estate's gamekeeper surveying his land. Although why he would carry an open rifle, I am not sure, so my friend will check with the landowner for me, as they did say listen and look out for everything around you and keep the curtains closed.

12:00 - He appears to have gone now, so fingers crossed that he will not return, as walking in the woods has become so very special for me. A concise trip into town is necessary to stock up on some provisions and almost instantly I notice how vast it now appears. The open fields and the expanse of this breathtaking scenery... I must have seen it hundreds of times, yet today I am seeing it with fresh eyes for the very first time. As we draw near to the town, the feeling of chaos comes into my energy field, the rushing of the people all heading for their destination. No time, it reminds me of Alice in Wonderland and the craziness of it all. I quickly source my provisions and my individual items of a sketch pad, highlighters and crayons, for the flowers are calling me to draw them in their splendor as they awaken for spring. I so want to retreat...retreat back into nature... the urge to return is quite astonishing for a Coventry city girl... and as we arrive back at The Shed, I breathe...PEACE.

THE WALK IN THE WOODS

Walking through the
woods again, it was a wondrous sight.
As I cast my eyes
across the valley in absolute delight.
Nine toads were seen
along the way, two with babies born.
For they carried them
upon their backs, to rest their weary paws.
Three butterflies and a bird
flew by, as the sound of the woodpecker tapped.
And as I gazed into the
forest deep…the sun came through the cracks.
It lights the heart of
every man or woman and child akin.
For in the light we too
can see, the velvety grass within.
This carpet covers our
wondrous earth, and keeps it warm and loved.
Ready for the start of
spring, and all of earth's beloved.
The Deer, the
Sheep, they are all here…
As I can
see their marks.
And as I leave
this path for now…
It is forever in my heart!!

As dusk is falling, my body speaks for it needs to eat and beckons an early night. I have prepared a simple dish of rice cooked with Turmeric, Quern pieces and mushrooms, cooked in the cold pressed coconut oil and my how delicious it tastes. Simple and yet more… if that makes sense, as it appears the less I do, the more it becomes, quite magical. I have studied today on and off and I feel safe in the knowledge and the wisdom that I am in the right place at the right time with the right people. For I am blessed with an intuition that I may hear the rumblings of God, Nature and the Universe, as it is spoken and guides the way home. My writings appear to be becoming less, maybe because I am, as I merge with my surroundings, it is like I am becoming less too.

The simple pleasures in life are delicious for sure and as I have such a feeling of love travelling all through my inner system, I am so grateful. I awaken again… this time with a burst of love within, such magnitude that it takes my breath away. For it is like a mighty waterfall as it ripples through me… over me, around me, within me as it consumes me… Like a crescendo, as it reaches its peak… the vibration makes my body shake and quiver… Then it slowly retreats leaving just the feeling of the hum… the peace so deep within. The power of Love. I look to the clock… only 10pm… still Day 9… just magical. I relax back into my pillow now, for I am so loved.

Good Night and God Bless for may the God-ness of the day stay with you. As the universe is a friend.

Always. X

DAY 10

Good Morning and God Bless for may the God-ness of the day be with you. As the universe is your friend.
Always.

Today I hear the Dawn Chorus again, but I drift back to sleep and do not emerge until 6:30. As I am up and about, I sit outside as usual with the birds and the one rabbit who appears to be joining us for our breakfast. I have filled their water bowls and placed bread on their tables... but the wind is strong today, very strong, so I decided to go for a walk at 7:00. As I wander through the woods, scattering seeds for the other birds along the way, I look at the flowers ready to draw their shapes and colours later on today and I notice a daisy with a pink edge. I cannot remember seeing a daisy with pink tips... Then as I arrive back to the shed, I hear the sound of the woodpecker as he drills away. I have not managed to see him yet, as I sit and slowly search the tree for his splendor. I look along the trunk, the branches and between the leaves but he is well and truly hidden. So I decided to try a different way and go within... chanting the OM and the RA, to dissolve the illusion through peaceful means... I meditate for a few minutes and speak in tongues, as the noise of the birds and woodpecker becomes louder. I am sure they can understand my prayers, as I speak in tongues and pray. I am asking the woodpecker to show himself to me. The strange sounds flow, which said...

'Where art thou woodpecker...
I can hear you so loudly...
But as I cannot see you... I pray.
Please show thyself to thee'.
And sure enough, as I open my eyes like magic, there he is

before me. Beautiful, just beautiful... as I watch him still at work and then I say again.

Thank You. Thank You. Thank You, for I am so grateful.

MESSAGE

Binoculars are suddenly shouted to me, at the weekend collect your binoculars. Okay I think to myself...will do and as I go to stand to collect something, what was it? Oh God in you I trust for I have not a clue, for the mind has escaped me again. Lol... Three people have walked by with a dog, one smiles as she sees me, the other waves as she too notices me and the last one shouts, for his dog is rushing to greet me. That is okay I say as she jumps all over me in a welcoming way. "One word from me and she does as she likes," he says, I laugh, for only humanity can think they are in control. The more I retreat, the more I appear to see in all ways, as the illusion is just that... an illusion.

Today I have to be honest, I am a bit niggled...trying to stay in my place and not engage elsewhere in my mind. But for some reason, I keep allowing my mind to drift back to situations from the past, back to people who I thought cared for me, and back to what seems like an injustice. (It's the advocate, the social worker rearing its head) Not injustice against me but against others, my friends and people I hold dear. I keep reminding myself it is not my business, for they may have their own lessons to learn.

ACCEPTANCE

Again... gosh this one is harder I feel than forgiveness, for in forgiveness I can understand but acceptance of behaviors I am struggling... so back to the drawing board for me and further prayers, as obviously I have much more to learn. The white flame will help me, for surely I must have been an idiot. Where was myself worth? And where was I when a friend decided to betray me, I should have told them straight there and then as soon as I realised. That drums up a sudden memory of a boyfriend who said… You have mug tattooed on your forehead in big letters, and his behaviour was less than desirable as he has gone on to spend most of his life in prison. What a waste really as my heart still goes out to people on repeat, for he had allowed his cycle of deprivation to influence him from his formative years. But a mug… not anymore for I refuse to partake in the illusion, I do not want to be the aspect of the fighter as I prefer to love and peace but… I respect myself enough now to say the boundary is firmly in place… this is like a cowboy western…the line is drawn! I think I must have watched too many of these films with my father in his last days… I may love you… but do not cross the boundary, especially if I am treating you with the respect and love that we all deserve, as I deserve to be treated the same way.

If people have genuinely learnt then, of course, you accept an apology, otherwise how can we ever be accepted for our mistakes but some are clever at hiding things and manipulate others to their own ends…as to keep repeating in different guises is not real, it is intentional.

I trust however and have faith as the illusion does eventually fall away, as foundations built on falsehood crumbles, so we all have to be prepared…prepared to be seen… not only by ourselves but by others and God of course. If the dark is hiding it will be shown, for the light is within us all… and it will shine upon itself, for it cannot be hidden forever… THE TRUTH WILL OUT as it says and I believe in the truth. A check in from a concerned friend, a flying visit to drop off cake..she just said as she left after all of a minute… "your eyes are blue today, really blue"… all change, what station are we heading to next? Tomorrow is my work day..and some people from the Cancer support group may drop by for Reiki, as I am not sure if they have been to the Garden Station before.

I love to see them as they have been very sweet to me and I like helping them where I can. Kindness is magical...I hear your words 'Keep the faith sister... keep the faith'. There could be new faces to meet too, so I shall not look back, or look forward any more, no more past niggles or future outcomes, just enjoy the moments. Right Tea and cake are beckoning...Yum. A walk in the woods and a small white feather appears on the path before me, so I stop to pick it up.

MESSAGE
Hold the Green Moldavite crystal and meditate. .. Shift...I remember it is in my purse from a while ago, so as soon as I return, I get it out. I decide to play some music as I have not listened to any for the past six days... Mother Divine by Craig Pruess and Ananda is what I need. Holding the Moldavite, I breathe the four-fold breath and begin to sink within... I am quickly shown a vision, a flash of Essex and a flash of Northumberland... North and South aligned with me in the middle. The 3, the triangle of the 'Holy Trinity'. We may work together at times, for some reason it appears as the return home will be as ONE in the 3.

I see myself with hands outstretched, taking the hand of one to the left and one to the right, with love for both, born out of many lifetimes spent together. A sudden deep breath emerges as if it has been stuck somewhere, as tears gently roll down my cheeks one by one.

REAL love, Gods love UNITED for the last time… It is like two halves of an egg, with me in the centre as the filling, the glue that binds it together for the good of all. Rejoice! For we have found our way, our light and our truth. May Peace be with you…both… we are sent to see through illusion… so that others may follow in the wake of our father's footsteps when they are ready. As LOVE leads the way… Always. I now play the Sacred Chants one… and relax by… Orenda Blu… Music is yet another source of beauty born of this world. After tea, I play some more songs and dance…I have not danced for what seems quite a while and as I sway and swoon, it is wonderful to be free. I speak of many things and I see so much more but nothing now can take me away from the path that I adore. A CD by Neil Diamond is ready to play and as I am drawn to look to the left, a piece of change I placed down on the table has stood up on its side… That is impossible I think as I look at the pound coin… standing upright! 'Miracles' come into mind, as the song blasts out… 'I'm a believer' Lol… so I dance again, all around the shed.

Life is good and I am enjoying the moments as they appear but now it's time for bed, as work tomorrow and I want to be well rested for whoever appears. As I have my lemon and Ginger tea in hand, I think if I were to toast us all before I retire… I would say. Love, Light, Laughter & many Blessings to us all… and Thank you for I am so grateful, as today has been another wonderful day.
The Universe is friendly to me.
Goodnight and God Bless.
Sleep well. Always x

I am awake again, only this time with the waves within that I know so well and to a song…

I can feel the difference as these are like the ones prior to your calls. Please God, this is not fair for it is not reciprocated... The deep love on a spiritual level through many lifetimes I can see and understand but the human one... why? Why do I suffer as it does not leave me... Am I not a faithful student and following my path, I can do no more... so please God spare me this... 'You are the first person I said I would want to see'... as you then said to me... after your time away when you rang with the urgency of a child. 'Wednesday' I replied. 'Wednesday I can see you', and you said no, can it not be sooner...

Why? For my mind cannot understand such confusion and as we walked and talked along the beachside after such a lovely day, you said "You were the first person I wanted to see." WHY?

As I held my hand to your heart and said this is impossible, for it is like a magnet; I now sit here shaking my head as it rears itself again. I almost want to shout Be gone... but I cannot, for the depth of love remains... Dear God as I pray whatever your plan is for me just make it swift for I may surely perish along the way, as I am not sure I have the strength to carry this, not this time.

Such is the depth that I have never known, it was hard enough before but again... Acceptance that is the only thing I can do and as I fall to my knees to pray. Please God help... I need to rest... for I have work to do tomorrow. And, as the message comes back to mind... Do not worry... for God will not give you anything that you cannot handle... I surrender.
Good Night and God Bless for may the God-ness of the day stay with you. As the universe is a friend.

Always. X

DAY 11

Good Morning and God Bless for may the God-ness of the day be with you. As the universe is your friend.
Always.

The second ones... new beginnings... OMG I barely open my eyes and it all kicks off a workday and back in the world, I switch on the phone and all go mad! Well, ACCEPTANCE is definitely the lesson I need to learn and I am being tested that is for sure as I can control nothing and no one. As soon as the phone goes on ping ping ping and the world is awake, virtually anyway on the internet, I think we have forgotten the beauty of the real world. Overnight occurrence... Now I knew, yesterday you said SHIFT but I did not quite comprehend the full scale of what was meant... now I do.

For overnight, my daughter whose home I had a room in, is moving near to her work, before I leave the shed so my room will be gone. The youngest has left to start her life with her boyfriend and has taken the dog, and my ex-husband has had enough, so he has put in for a transfer to escape to his mother 250 miles away. Jesus...I'm not swearing... I am telling you... it is like a flipping sitcom, your having a laugh...

Well in the blink of eye things can change... I am technically homeless (for real), and now this shed looks even more appealing. Today I need to completely surrender and hand it all over to GOD, for one thing sure enough there is nothing at present I can do about anything, as I am in the middle of my 40 days 40 nights. Have faith sister... I have a small reprieve as I am house sitting for one week at the barn on my return from here but where to put my stuff? What was left of it anyway, I have not got a clue. Clothes, crystals and my books, my whiteboard, my Buddha my angel, my various work tools I have more than I think for my work, perhaps they can stay at this workplace, for now at least. Dick Whittington... maybe I shall have to join you with a suitcase or a backpack...honestly a bit of warning would have been good... oh well I suppose you did say SHIFT. I am going for breakfast... at least I can control that.

As I feed the birds and walk in the woods, I remember the message 'God would not give you anything that you could not handle'. Okay, I trust and have faith, as you know what you are doing. I pull a few cards on my return and they reiterate trust, divine guidance and destiny. Until I surrender everything entirely, it appears I am allowed to keep nothing.

I am booking an interview with a Buddhist wise man Lama Yeshe who sits in a multi-faith centre in the borders of Scotland, as I can speak with him freely about my life, as it has changed direction so rapidly in this past two years: so perhaps only those who have trodden this path before me, can truly understand. I am settling down a bit now as the realisation... all is well... Is retaking hold in my system, I have good friends and people around me, so I know I am okay.

You would think by now that I am used to sudden change, but it still jolts me. I feel it is because of an incident in the past that I did not expect, that same feeling appears to arise when a sudden change occurs.

'Know thyself well' Tracy...It is not the past, it is the present and the present has many gifts... not just the one. People keep saying you are brave. I could not do what you are doing, everything is relative depending upon your chosen path and life experiences. I do not feel that what I am doing is brave at all, as many face real danger out there in the world daily... war-torn communities... abuse etc... etc. I am so fortunate not to be one of them, so I am truly blessed. As I write this someone has just come in to speak with me who has very recently lost his wife... only in his fifties if that, so you see everything in life is relative.

He is very genuine and felt drawn to the place last week when we first met, so we sat together today and chatted and it was good to share experiences... as he too has experienced the loss of a great teacher in his life, and has previously completed a silent retreat for himself. He could understand everything that I have been experiencing and I him. It is funny how people are drawn together when circumstances are similar, as I do not believe in coincidences, and know that we are all connected in some way to assist each other.

Tonight I shall pray for him as he needs assistance at this time. God Bless him and the rest of the world who are in suffering. There are many things in the world that humanity cannot control, so we all have to learn this lesson in one way or another... Acceptance... as a friend once said to me and as quoted by Mother Teresa "If you find yourself homeless one day just accept it" I understand that now. Things are already beginning to pan out one by one... as I let go and allow God the Universe to support me, for I am not alone and I am learning all the time in one way or another, for I will always be the student and the teacher.

I have surrendered and I promise to have an adventure, as I think about an up and coming trip I have planned. I can get from Suffolk by a lift to Epping... for the train to London and then from London to Newcastle by coach: all for around £12 now that's a bargain! I have learnt that already today. Lol... life can be fun, I must let go of the reigns more often… haha. One day in the not too distant future, I feel I will be completely free… just amazing. A friend comes back to mind as we hug under the umbrella and the feeling of Love abounds, anyone who is with you will be fortunate they say… I was the lucky one. For only when you have loved and lost, can you truly understand its meaning but ACCEPTANCE is the lesson for today so 'accept' I will.

Pride has never really been my thing as I can apologise, forgive myself and others and I am an excellent honest, open-hearted communicator but not all are the same and I have to accept that too so I will continue to love unconditionally as I always have. I am always here… for no one should ever fear me, as I will always talk to you with love no matter what the outcome.

A short one today as I have nearly lost my mind… I can feel the mind pulling like a tension at the middle of the forehead… the third eye… the energy pulls and pulls because the mind is not in control and it struggles as it wants to be.

MESSAGE
Accept and be free. POP
As more and more shifts occur, the eyesight changes and becomes misty again… another memory when you said from many miles away 'I am going blind' Lol… Watch what you say, as you were…blind to the silly people around you who did not love you like I did and did not have your best interests at heart, for they were in it for their own selfish ends of many things. God bless you, I know how hard this one is, as I have been there many times ..for all of us have to go through the process of learning including myself. The number 7 in numerology is the destiny path, not just for myself but for you too and this is what I have discovered so I will share it

here, for it has been beneficial to know. I love the use of numbers now as the universe is mathematical, as is the earth, as above as below, as science is beginning to prove.

So now I use numerology in my readings like Swami to look at each person's DOB and destiny... How funny we both have the same number from birth, even when I married it did not change, as it still worked out the same... thank you I was blessed for I could never be taken off my path.

A number 7 should use analysis and research to find the truth for themselves in life, as opportunities for self-development present along the way as they are destined to find good things... The real treasure, however lies within, so while information may come to you from many sources, dig deep and find the beauty of all aspects of self and others.7 has the gift of insight and can use their intuition in order to assist them in overcoming obstacles and moving forward. The 7 path is that of gaining understanding and investigating and searching for inner wisdom for they are the sage. They have the knowledge within but need to access it, to overcome blockages by trusting their gut instincts, learn to trust your intuition and find the golden nuggets of information which are the answers to questions which may arise along the path. Meditation and tools that open you up to seeing the truth from many perspectives will help a 7, so as an understanding begins to occur, follow the steps that you feel are right in your heart and allow the flow of knowledge to grow from within.

Before I retire, I feel that we all need to realise that nothing is ever black and white or set in stone and just because it appears to be this way, one day it can change for change is good...we all need to be flexible, open, honest and loving... we can ask for help, as this is not a weakness, it is actually a strength... in the realisation of ourselves as we learn to know ourselves well then the world will soon become a better place for us all.

The Owl is hooting, so that is my cue to go to bed these days, just as the dawn chorus is my cue to wake up, when we live by the law of nature and not by man-made rules for a while, we are able to see much more of what is truly real... for the illusion fades and the truth emerges... in the light of love, faith and trust in the divine. Do not be scared to go within or look in the mirror, for it is fantastic... once seen, as the bits, you do not like you can change for it is never too late.

Good night and God Bless, I am so grateful for the day I have had today as I have been forced to look deeper within and release more that no longer serves me and I can see the genuineness of the friendship that surrounds me.

May the God - Ness of the day stay with you. The universe is a friend.

Always X

DAY 12

Good Morning and God Bless for may the God-ness of the day be with you. As the universe is your friend.
Always.

A lovely day of sunshine and song as I wake up again to the birds and the rush of love within. It is another work day and I am more relaxed today, as the feeling of trust embeds itself even deeper within me. The cakes are cooking in the cafe at the Garden Station and the smell of home-cooked soup and scones flow... I chat and laugh with the owners and know how blessed I am to be here, for their genuine concern for me is evident and their care so loving. A sudden thought fleets through my mind... You should be a part of all this you know... I have always shared with you. It is lovely to watch people come and go with their dogs too as they are allowed to bring them here, for these people love animals as they too are unconditional and know they are part of one's family. People come to see the garden to chat, arrange weddings, parties events etc., such a magical place of love and now a healing centre too, as they have taken me into their space, after all we were drawn together by the universe. A friend calls by with flowers for me and I take her into the Tiny Healing Room as I call it, she looks around and says it is lovely Tracy, full of light and love, for she can feel the energy.

I am so very fortunate and I know that, so I am always so so grateful... As the day progresses and people leave, it is time for me to go to see my granddaughter for I have not seen her since my silent retreat and I am hoping to catch her for an hour before her bedtime. I am given a lift and as I walk in... her face...it lights up the room as she waves her little hand and shoots up from the sofa. Hi, Nan... Nan Hi, she says so sweetly as I hug her so tight, and nearly cry... for the love I feel for this little child is immense, for she is another wise and beautiful soul. I have to watch Peter Pan and Happy Feet, Read books, Paint and hold onto Woody and Elsa from frozen...she knows what to do and how to make me hers in every way... children are so special, open-hearted and full of love, how things can change from birth to adulthood.

As I go to leave, I can see her apprehension as she hugs me goodbye, I am coming back do not worry little one for my heart is full of love for you and I can never leave, not really. I am following my path and may even go away at times but I will always return for you are in my heart and our lives are entwined... We must have chosen each other before we came and now when we are here we must share those special times always, for life is too short. And if I ever upset you, tell me and let us clear it up straight away, for our time together is precious...Today will be a short journal, for the pace of life has entered and taken me away on business and in dealings with others. However now I am back at The Shed... the night has drawn in and as I stand and just stare in awe at the night sky... the stars are out in their hundreds. So bright, so beautiful, so many complex patterns and systems... how could this have all been formed and created out of a big bang?

It is an intricate system designed somehow... mind-blowing when you see its beauty and feel its love in your heart. I am so grateful... the owl is hooting again and I am ready for sleep, as my body is telling me to rest.

Good Night and God Bless for may the God-ness of the day stay with you. As the universe is a friend.

Always. X

DAY 13

Good Morning and God Bless for may the God-ness of the day be with you. As the universe is a friend.
Always.

13, unlucky for some or could be new beginnings, as watched over by the Angels... and the three for Holy Trinity. Last night, I must admit I was little on edge as I wanted to sit outside and watch the stars for longer but I suddenly felt that I was being watched... with interest. My eyes could not adjust deeper into the wood for the light had blinded me and as I felt into the darkness, I could pinpoint where I thought you were and my body went into fight or flight! Like the Deer with the senses all on heightened alert...I stood still and linked in. Now I wish I was that Owl and able to see within all the shadows, the shadows of the trees and all around me, so I go within myself and listen even deeper, calling on all my senses. For the moonlight is lighting me up so bright and as I am wearing white, I must look like a ghostly apparition; or an Angel of the Light.

A memory suddenly shoots into my mind as I hear my father's voice as he says... "It's not the dead you need to worry about, it's the ones who are alive". And although I used to laugh at this, right now at this moment...it could be true, for I am linking in and realising that this person could be so. As they are used to blending in and walking the woods at night, they know how to move around and keep right out of sight.

The human race is one that may decide to harm, for the gift and curse of free will is there and could be used in any way, as they perceive themselves to be, the good man or the hunter? As I link in more, I think which are you? Friend or foe... only time will tell for sure now I have been discovered. This morning as I hear the first bird and the song that I have grown to love, it is with such happiness that I feed them all as we have our breakfast. I do wish they would come closer though, as my thoughts of Scotland and Kielder drift back in…I love them so much for they are very dear to me. The sun is breaking though and all feels well, I have to go into town today and my heart drops for the busy scenes that await me and the energy field is not one that I relish now; but I will do my best to smile and hope that my light helps someone else today.

A toad passes by and I laugh, for a conversation with the owner comes to mind as I read her my poem at the weekend 'The walk in the woods'. At first she begins to wipe her eyes, as she says that has made me feel quite tearful… .it had hit her heart… But then as time passes she must have been thinking about the toads, as she suddenly said," Tracy, that is really weird because in all my 63 years I have never seen a toad carry its babies." Well, they must have been I said for there was three or four on one toad's back. Which are the females again I ask? The large ones she says. Yes, that's right the mother!

Well… with that she laughs and says, Tracy!!! Its spring… and as it takes a few seconds to register with me…we both roar with LAUGHTER… as she says in a rich Somerset accent "The dirty Buggers" Well for now, I can hardly breathe…for we are laughing so hard… OMG, I said I will have to change the poem. But then I think… no leave it…for the ones who realise will laugh at my innocence, as I wander the woods with the eyes and the heart of a child in wonder. "Oh, dear!" I say, shaking my head, God needs to have a word with Miss Toad… for she cannot love herself… one partner at a time, please. Where are your morals, ethics and boundaries, Miss Toad and although I do still love her beauty, I think I definitely prefer Swans.

As I sit with my tea and my book on Eastern Philosophies, I start to feel jolts in my body, for I am reading about things I know and understand which I have seen myself and wrote about in Journals, for I am not a learned scholar... I have not studied the philosophies, yet I know How? How are they resonating so strongly with me? Is it a deep resonance and inner knowledge/wisdom through many many lives lived... for how would I know as I can feel it in my heart so strongly as the truth? The feeling of love suddenly rushes through my physical body with waves like ecstasy, as my inner soul signature recognises it all. Dropping my attention to my feet and slowly breathing my energy back to the centre, as it floods through me again and makes me shake.

With that, I look to the side of me and a Robin is now close by, he feeds eagerly with his beak while he watches me closely with his eyes. Come, come near I say for I will never harm you. It is beautiful to watch his little face and colours so bright, for the full red chest, his tiny legs and delicate claws like fingers, so intricate and beautiful... just like a newborn baby, a joy to watch close up. As I continue to read the stories of Saints and Angels alike, I know the Angels are real for I have seen one.

The memory of this day flashes before me from 2005... I remember it well for how could I ever forget. That night I woke up and crept down the stairs, throwing myself onto Gods Heart... as I stretched out my arms along the mantelpiece and rested my head. I cried from the very depths of my being... and it was like I was being crucified for I could take no more. I had reached the end of the road and there was no other way out for me… but death, for in that second I made a decision to end my life.

I had always not understood suicide but at that moment it felt the only way, for everything had left me. My faith, my hope, my trust in all humanity and I did not want to carry on. As I write this now, tears well for I have never shared this with my family and I am filled with love for God, The Angels and for my blessed children, for I had at that moment forgotten them all as I only thought of myself.

But in that second I truly understood the feeling of suicide and for all that have succumbed to this way, I bless you so much, for they know not what they do… All of a sudden I felt a weight of something being placed around my shoulders and pulled so very very tight, it had warmth like a thick blanket and as it tightened further I could feel a love… a feeling of LOVE awash...like no other that I had ever experienced.

At first, I thought my husband had heard my sobs and had come to see me but as this feeling was not like anything that I had ever known or recognised, I gently lifted my head. As I turned it to the right, I saw with my own eyes...something tall and broad with bright white feathers like wings wrapped around me holding me so tightly, as I was unable to move.

THE ANGEL
I saw it, for it was real… and the love I felt so true.
So now I could never kill myself, for I believed in you.
For whatever reason, I was spared, and from that day to this.
I made a commitment to my path and the road that leads to bliss.
I love you now, the same as then, and that can never die…
For once it registers, in the heart, it is eternally alive!

One in a million chance comes to mind as I read that without a teacher.

It is a one in a million chance that anyone can reach enlightenment.

But as my father's words ring in my ears...I know I will give it my best shot, for he said you can do anything Tracy if you put your mind to it. OR as in this case maybe... empty the mind... to nothingness in the sacred space.

A memory suddenly flashes by... "Cystic Fibrosis, your baby has," the consultant says."Have you heard of it? He will probably only live until he is about sixteen years of age.""What is the chance of a woman from Coventry meeting a man in Norfolk and us having a child with Cystic Fibrosis?" I said... "Oh," he replied "... probably a million to one!!"

Another statement flashes through, this time from a good friend as he says to me... You are rare Tracy, very rare... A mysterious one... Thank you, for now that is taken as a compliment... The chosen business name fleets in Universal Harmony, or Inner Guru Propagator as a woman once said, who experienced my retreat in Assisi. Now I wonder at it all, for there is really only 'THE ONE'. As all roads lead to home, so we can never really get lost. I had to nip into town today as my son was ill, so I had the baby for a few hours and as I walked her through the park sitting and observing, the feeling of being a round peg in a square hole emerges as I watch society, as they all go about their business. All on different parts of the same path, all rushing here and there...where ever their understanding is regarding themselves, as they pass by and I hear their conversations... so many of which I've had too over the years.

Nothing can be changed and there is nothing for me to do but care about myself right now and then you. This experience has already changed me and for that, there is no doubt that I will not return from this place the same... I know that now.

Know Thyself Well my friends, Know Thyself Well.

Tiredness is beginning to take hold after my time back in the world, so tomorrow I can completely rest and withdraw into the fold. God's Love and energy abounds for me and the balance is coming too, for this time in the world I did not feel the vibration of the smack so severely through my body. My energy was held at the feet as I observed it all, by keeping myself in my place of centre... as I moved around in the world, still yet in motion if that makes sense.

My business is mine and mine alone and I need to remember that. Loving, Kindness and Compassion of course, is vital for those that suffer still but I cannot make it my business or interfere in free will for it is theirs alone. It will be lovely when you come bearing your good news and have a smile so bright, for we will surely delight... in such engagement.

I am blessed for day 13 has been a little challenging at times but also a real joy, so I suppose that is a balance and I am nearer yet again to the lesson of Acceptance.

Good Night and God Bless for may the God-ness of the day stay with you. As the universe is a friend.

Always. X

DAY 14

Good Morning and God Bless for may the God-ness of the day be with you. As the universe is a friend.
Always.

Well, I am well rested... as I slept for 12 hours! I did hear the Dawn Chorus but I drifted back to sleep with the beautiful sound of the bird song.

BALANCE

This must have been how it was, for 24 hours in a day. Living in nature to nature's clock and not to the man-made time... Eating from the land in season, only taking what we needed and not in greed. Connecting with each other in communities, listening to the wisdom and communicating with God. Wonderful! Not a bad life for the one in the shed. I brought my special T pot along for the journey that was a gift from my first born son, a glass one with the mesh in the middle for the loose tea leaves and I borrowed a china cup and saucer.

Cheers... for I have posh tea in the shed. Fun... life can be so, if we make it that way. I was dreaming again with a 'Vision' as I awoke to the remembrance and the seeing of specific details. A friend I was holding tightly in my arms as he could feel the love and as I held them close I said you have come home to the mother... that is what it is. And as I finished speaking a rib appeared out of mid-air and was handed to me. It shook me, for I awoke immediately with a jolt and the thought of the father was given, of which this person is also a father as I am a mother.

I saw the mother and the father standing together as one and the waves of Ecstasy had returned during the vision, for God's Love I am certain is the purest of all. The Mother and Father within… the Alpha and the Omega. I will have to look now to the scriptures today, because did it not say somewhere that God made a woman out of Adams' rib? More to learn obviously…it will be another good day today. 'I can feel it in my bones' Lol… as the older generation used to say. I love the funny old sayings… The feeling… that the philosophy of which I speak of has been born and is growing…just as this book has become, like a good seed that was obviously planted some time ago within and in the completion of the rest of this 40 days, the steps will appear as some are already here.

Can you imagine if all our communities, towns, cities and villages were in balance?

Eco-friendly housing. Organic food is grown on the land and sold between cities, shared as they should be. Skill sets coming together everywhere for the greater good of the planet. Workplaces being in balance, good food being eaten for lunch rest areas and a work-life balance. The world would shift dramatically and it would not take long if everyone did their bit… within and then without. Humanity would be happy for Balance and Love in the hearts of all would reign.

As within, as without, as above, as below… The flow of life like water in all its goodness and God-Ness the creation. Even as I write, the flow is startling… the waves, the feeling of the waterfall, as the soul signature is so happy and my writing has changed again as it flips back into scripture italic style… fluid. All good but what about fear?

FEAR…This fear that infects our consciousness, why do we allow it in, when we can use our free will to plant the good seeds instead. A noticing occurred yesterday and I forgot to document it as the world outside took over… During the time I had my grandchild for a few hours yesterday. We received a call from my daughter for she is making a brave step, especially for her, out into the unknown. She wobbled… and threw herself into lack, which then rippled out like a pebble in the pond.

Then I flipped over like a coin and placed myself into lack, which then also rippled out like a pebble in the pond. Can you see the pattern? For you see from 1 it soon became 3, affected by the fear but as I stand in my knowledge and wisdom so far, this was turned around as quickly as I could manage to with love, as I know how this works now, so I have to be the one to take the lead and the responsibility for myself. For we are all learning, we are all processing and we are all on our own unique and individual authentic paths back to the light.

Remember the message?
Love and compassion are needed for yourself and others, for kindness is magical! How did we all connect before mobile phones and the internet? Things progress and rightly so for they have to but where are the letters, the writings, we do not seem to receive them anymore. Emails are the closest I suppose but even then they are not the same, for the letters were full of news shared with family and friends. The love, the care for each other… it used to be wonderful to receive such a thing.

Progress ok…but do not forget the old ways too, when we used to have such kinship, the community, the love for each other as neighbours. Send the letter, visit, pop in for tea and cake, and surprise a friend. Be the love that will reign again in the world. Someone said to me the other day... Today has not been a good day for me because I only had 3. I said in reply, NO it has been a good day today... For you have had 3. Those 3 will go away and tell 1, then you will have 6.

Those 6 will go away and tell 1,then you will have 12.

Those 12 will go away and tell 1,then you will have 24.

SO, can you not see? You have had a good day!

Do not buy into the illusion. Remember always to watch what you are telling yourself and see the bigger picture, plant those good seeds within yourself and all that you meet. 3 is a good number really because it is Angelic, a good day I feel was had by one and all. Jesus the loaf and the fish comes to mind for it multiplied, miracles happen, you just have to believe them, feel them in your heart with love and set yourself free.

For do not wait, it isn't coming, t is here NOW in the 'present', the GIFT of life on this amazing planet, so enjoy it all in the now moments.

The sun is breaking through and as I glance at my watch, not that I need time really but my body is speaking for I have been writing and I need to eat. I am late said the hare in Alice in wonderland... Lol, Crazy world.

MEDITATION... and a vision of a place once visited where good work is completed in faith, as the heart of love continues within many there. But some are in it for their own glory and that is sad, as I feel there are missing out on the very thing they are supposed to be sharing. It was during the mediation that the face of a friend from this place was shown as they were thinking of me and the wave's return, as they are genuine in God's Love.

Now I wonder if they see the truth of their situation yet, for they are never stuck with anything or anyone if they truly believe... Love in action... is God in action, not human desire. So I am hoping this is what was meant, for they have worked so hard and deserve the best possible support around them, for they are truly following their path. Their heart is known, believe in miracles... for when I last prayed for assistance at their place of worship, something occurred, not that it needs to be in an area, for it can be anywhere, if our heart is connected... a park, a bench, the beach, your home, anywhere..for trinkets are only trinkets, God's love is real in the heart.

It is just that the feeling of the chapel is loved and the energy of my friend that prays there regularly, for it is palpable so I like to visit occasionally. My granddaughter likes it as well, for she never moves but sits still and watches as I pray and meditate. She too can feel the energy and she loves to walk the grounds with me. On this particular day, I had prayed for a Miracle for a friend who I was truly concerned about, I had prayed for them around five months beforehand, in one of the chapels of St Francis, so this was my second time of asking and as the tears flowed from my heart to that of God, I prayed that it had been heard.

We were walking outside together after visiting and as she took my hand to show me the trees and the snowdrops... all of a sudden I could see the Mother Mary, in a vision in my mind's eye, for it was like a film of her standing in front of me. I was frozen to the spot for a second but she was definitely there... for she said Miracles happen and then disappeared. Before these 40 days, I have been left wondering... but I suppose it will be shown when the time is right, for in the Divinity I believe... 'Divine Timing' is heaven sent and not man-made, for we are not in control, no matter what or who we think we are.

So, I will say Thank you now for I am truly grateful. The woods have been wonderful again today and I have walked them a few times finding another little white feather along the way, funnily enough, it was in my palm as I had placed it inside my glove just before mediation on the grass. I had forgotten this... My mind has been escaping me all day today as I really do struggle to think now... A lay down was hard for a little while, as the waves were rising and falling throughout me and the dizziness returned. As I linked into the consciousness earlier to try and see where it was coming from. I could feel an angst... like a frustration and I knew it was not mine; for it feels like that of a friend struggling with something. So I sent my love and compassion, for free will is the menace at present. However, as I get up to walk again in the woods, I feel all is well...as they are loved. Earlier, I realised that yesterday I had put in only one earring in the left ear and had gone to town that way... Lol... There may be the day I go out with different shoes on! Today I noticed later that I had placed the earring in my right ear... hilarious what is happening? At least I suppose it was balanced out.

Then finally, I managed to actually put them both in, thank goodness true balance at last. I also walked to get something... many times today! And if I just knew what on earth the something was, it would be genuinely beautiful for it has completely escaped me.

I keep laughing at myself, for it must be a comedy to watch, a good sketch for any writer. A noticing... Oh, no CATASTROPHE... I have no clean socks!!! See I'm still a pampered princess, nature hasn't quite tamed me yet. I decided to cook a lovely meal and I have enjoyed all of everything today immensely, it is already 12 hours since I awoke and the body is wanting to rest. The darkness must determine the clock, for usually I manage to stay up at least another two hours of man-made time... Who am I to question, for during this time here, I've just surrendered to whatever is meant for me and I love it all so far... so thank you for I am so grateful that the universe is friendly to me.

I hope all your dreams come true... of the good seeds. Good Night and God Bless for may the God-ness of the day stay with you. As the universe is a friend.

Always. X

DAY 15

Good Morning and God Bless for may the God-ness of the day be with you. As the universe is a friend.
Always.

I awoke with the Dawn chorus and immediately remember my dream.
...
DREAM
Meeting with an old friend as we catch up, drink tea and listen eagerly to each other's experiences.

But then we are interrupted as my ex-husband walks into the room, Oh, Crikey I think not again… Have you nowhere to go? I say, as he laughs and leaves.

Mothers and Fathers everywhere, see what you do? For the early formative years, shape the adults out there in the world. MEN - A child or an overprotective father. Where is the balance…

Women are not subordinate to men, for God is good and created all equally in balance, who slipped that bit in the bible? For it was not God, I am sure. Man can look after a woman if it suits them both but it must be a shared decision and not of control, as nothing but genuine love and kindness will bring out the absolute best in her, Unconditional love.

For myself as a woman that would never bow down to a man in ego, yet if you were to treat me with the Heartfelt Love, Respect and Kindness, as God created you in his good image, then you will taste the sweetest of all... that you have ever known, of unconditional love for I know it's the truth.

WOMEN - Watch what you do... balance. Are you the child or the overprotective mother? Treat man with the unconditional love, compassion and kindness that God created in you. Then see him work in earnest, for he will surely please you. Neither is subordinate, so do not raise your voices or your hands but love each other with all your hearts and you will both reach the promised land. The only one to bow down too in Love, is the creator, The Lord. Bow your heads to him and be grateful in thought, word and deed for he has given us such a wonderful gift. As I write these words, a song starts to build... and as I catch its words, the message and song come through together.

MESSAGE - Know Thyself Well. Alleluia.....
For those in same-sex partnerships, these principles still apply, for we are both male and female within... The whole.

DREAM.
My friend, as I see him now in his entirety. He is so happy, joyous of my company as I am with him. His eyes twinkle with unconditional love... He is authentic as something happens and he sees to it, for he is independent and does not need me to step in, for he is not a child, he is a man and he is 'whole' again. A beautiful dream, so lovely to see for it is RARE.

MEDITATION / MESSAGE
Honour Thy Mother and Thy Father...
Do not speak ill of the dead, for they have tried their best with what they knew and thought they understood. Know Thyself Well

A sudden thought emerges… The Twin Flame Phenomena. Now perhaps my understanding is that there could be more than one twin flame, as this depends upon the frequency that you are vibrating on and I appear to be finding two of everything at the moment. Two white feathers now on my walk like twins… so I place them on my Mesa Alter, light a candle ready to pray. Soul mates… there are many.

Karmic relationships… there are many, as you work to release yourself from the lessons and the layers of the onion to reach your core. But the Soul Signature, your own true self twin, in a sense the Eternal Flame Within is YOU. For your soul seeks itself in the union, as you are both the Mother and the Father. In a way this contradicts but the feeling is once 'Whole'. As you are 'Wholeness' you are 'Holiness' and it finds itself like a magnet, sticking together no matter what, as the Trinity returns to God in its Goodness and balance.

The 3, I feel is the Mother, the Father and the spark of Christ… I will ask and see if the answer is given but somehow that feels right. Someone has just got a message to me to say that a good friends father has just passed away, so I break my silence for a few moments as they are suffering and turn on my phone so I can send them so much love for it is needed at this time.

Bless you, my friend, for I know this pain and it is great… but you are strong and you are a wonderful person, you have been a good daughter and you are a true friend, so you are very very loved. X

***

In meditation, I keep seeing who at first I think is myself, then who looks like my mother, then my father and then an older woman who feels like me. This has been seen many times before my silence and throughout this time, so now I am beginning to realise they are showing myself as The Wise Sage... The Wise Woman who has lived before so many times. For over lifetimes, we refine and refine until eventually, as Swami said to me, we lose the parts that no longer serve us, as he said I had lost mine. For he did not know but when I was told to kneel at the stream, they did say I was free... that my karma had been spent and now I was to enjoy the rest of my days and be free to do as I please.

My path has not been easy and as past regressions have shown, I have been hurt so many times but I know that I too have hurt others, however in my learning along the way, I still managed to keep my heart open, in unconditional love. I truly believe this is the key to the kingdom of heaven on earth, as we change and grow within ourselves and be the light there is in the world for all humanity. I always forgive as I forgive myself too, so I continue to love you, for if you treat me well and with much love, you will have it all returned to you in cart loads, in unconditional love.

But if not, then please just keep away for now, for if you cannot treat me as you would want to be treated, then something is misaligned. And as God says if we are truly sorry, then of course we can return, for no one is ever turned away... the door is never closed, as we have to look within and be honest with ourselves and then the truth will be exposed... as we will be liberated. We are in a human body and we do make mistakes...for that I surely know but now I am trusting in the Lord and hoping my soul can continue to evolve in God's Love and evolve until the day I too shall return to the heart of God forever.

My Gratitude is so heartfelt... but I know that you know this, for it is felt and not told, for in the creation we are all transparent as the illusion is not real... and every thought, word and deed is felt in the heart of Christ, so we cannot hide, not even from ourselves, as the light will eventually turn inwardly as we learn to 'Know Thyself Well'.

To some this will be controversial, as I now say again that I am not religious, yet some will understand... I am spiritual... As I Love God, The Truth and do not seek to control but to empower others in their freedom to become their authentic selves. Religion can feel in such a way with the sameness of politics... does it seek to control in some way? As that I am sure was not the intention.

For the truth was told and it was for us all to live in Peace, Joy and Unconditional Love, 'As One'. To share and care for each other as ourselves and I pray that one day this will all return to earth.

As I check in with myself every day and say in absolute honesty... How are you doing today? If great...CONGRATULATE and if not so good, FORGIVE. Look in the mirror in love and back to basics, start again, peeling back the layers as we can always start over. For every day is a new day, every hour is a new hour, every minute is a new minute and every second is a new second...until we are at core and time is no more. X

As I walk the woods I cry for the suffering of my friend, the loss of her father so dear and as it rears its head for me, I know I was truly blessed, for I was able to resolve our differences before my father's passing, in so much love. My thoughts fleet across to another friend who struggles at times to see the pattern, for they may be living within a similar situation as I did.

But then as I link with their heart for they are good, I cry again, for their open-hearted love towards their father is known. How could anyone have ever hurt you, I cry from the very depths of my soul, especially as a child? For you were as beautiful and gentle a soul then, as you are now.

But I know he loves you, for you have forgiven him... and one day you will realise that... for he knew not what he did. God Bless you for I know the pain that comes again but in Christ spark within us all I do believe... and I believe in you.
With all my love always X
I keep going hot and cold today... like I have the flu.

As I have been in study for most of today and I am now feeling more blessed than ever before... for the fear that has been installed into the hearts and minds of people across the ages must have been man-made, or mans misperception of the word of God; for no one can make me believe that God is not good and that he will punish me.

For if he forgives all that sin and sees straight into our hearts, then he must see work in goodness in his name too and the truth of all situations. The glory seekers, I realise are sometimes working from a place of vanity, for they wish to be adored for their own names sake and not yet realising that the spirit of God is working through them as a facilitator. For they are only a vessel of blood and matter... but that is just ego as it reigns within and they are not yet down to the core... but one day they will see the truth... the truth of themselves.

I had a message once when I felt so low, for I thought I was indeed being punished in some way when it was said... You have done far more good in your life than you have ever done bad. The right people are in the right place, at the right time and for the right reasons, so just have faith, and they were... for I have been saved before not just once but many times. So if I am completely on the wrong road, then someone is definitely having a laugh.

I have been led to so many good people on my travels through intuition and visions, who have treated me as their own, with kindness, love and compassion, so if that is at the hands of the devil, then so be it for he must love me. Good Lord, I say... help man to see through their own illusion.
Another mindful walk in the woods and the singing of the song... Alleluia Alleluia Alleluia.

A prayer in nature as the birds sing around me, as dusk draws near... I speak in tongues and ask the Good Lord for assistance, as I also link in with the Ascended Masters Buddha, Say Baba and Ganesh for they are all so beautiful. And I thank them all in so much gratitude... As today has been yet another wonderful day and as sit in nature more and more, the outside world appears to fall away.

A small meditation... As I light a candle incense and relax, I can feel the flow within and I squeeze the back of my neck for a few seconds, as it feels as though something is trying to push through...at the junction, the main station. Now my eyes feel as though the muscles behind them are pulling, trying to roll the eyes over to look deeper inside, as I can feel the waves. I can see within my own darkness and my light for as the owl hoots, it is nearly time.

The feeling of love begins to swirl within as I cast my soul out into the hands of God for my next steps… For I am in service… and I know the ending of my days will be in poverty, for I have promised that all I earn will be distributed as the time comes. But for now, they said Abundance is mine in every way and I accept, for I know that I can receive… in all things… in God's Love, for the continuation of my journey but not a coin, a note or anything will enter through the gate to the kingdom of God… for only what is in my 'heart' can I carry with me.

Enjoy the moments… In Joy.

A meal fit for a Queen was eaten tonight, as I tasted its flavour, only a simple stir fry with greens, bean sprouts, onion and mushrooms. But as I added a few special ingredients of walnuts, cashews and coconut oil to the mix…the rich deliciousness of it all, burst my taste buds, for as life is truly alive, as it too is rich in flavour… Thank you. Thank you. Thank you.

For the first time tonight, I could just relax with a little TV… something that I do not have but a nature documentary perhaps, or another land that I have not yet visited. Oh well, I can visit these in my dreams for now and travel far and wide, for the delights of this earth are many and I am truly blessed.

Bread and Butter pudding with sultanas and Italian honey is beckoning me now…Ooh, such earthly pleasures… Lol… then BED. The hum of Peace within… .the heart thuds and silence… deeper and deeper it goes as the water flows… My mind appears to have left me again as I cannot think but actually now I realise, I do not really need to, and for each day is a new level of surrender to the divine… In trust and love.

Good Night and God Bless for may the God-ness of the day stay with you. As the universe is a friend.

Always x

DAY 16

Good Morning and God Bless for may the God-ness of the day be with you. As the universe is a friend.

The sun is breaking through and it is a lovely day, the Dawn Chorus rang but as I heard it, I was also feeling again the rumbles of thunder, the crashing of waves and the sweet bird song, all within my system. This is the third morning when I have awoken to this…it has been on and off over the past two years, sometimes regularly, daily like this and other times intermittent but what I am noticing now is that they are increasing in their intensity.

For these happenings are outside of my control… this is nothing man made, for it is a feeling of love felt like no other, for it cannot be explained but I will try my best to set the scene. I did leave a note last night just in case because surely I may die from this… or at least fall into some sort of deep meditation like asleep, for it appears to take me and I am helpless.

Sleeping Beauty may be found after all… just make sure you fetch that prince… for only true loves kiss will set her free… These happenings appear to start like the waves I have described within, they build and build and the body is helpless against it. No strong woman or man can fight it, as the physical body is like a small waft of paper in the strongest of winds… My body unfurls as I sleep in a ball and then it straightens itself out quickly, flipping me onto my back as the waves grow in intensity. The crashing, the ebb and the flow like the sea, as the waves crash to the shore, the waterfall as it cascades over the rocks, so strong that it knocks everything out of its way, for nothing can defeat it… as it rushes down the mountain.

Then it changes for... the gentleness of the summer breeze, the sun as it kisses your face, your eyes, your lips so tenderly and the gentlest of stokes across your skin. And it makes the body shudder My body flips like a fish out of the water as it jumps about and is thrown around like a rag doll...for it is truly defenseless, it can do NOTHING, for the body is in the depths and the grip of SURRENDER.

All of my chakras are alive...tingling from the SOLE of each foot, over the toes, up through the body, out of the PALMS of the hands and throughout each cell, each energy particle of my very being alight like a bright light, to the depths of my core. It happens over and over again for I cannot wake up, yet my consciousness is aware of all the sensations... it devours me until it stops with a deep thud of the heart, as I rest in the arms of the beloved. It used to exhaust me but now it appears I am energized as coupled with nature I am in the greatest place of Peace and Love in the deep, deep hum of the OM. As I survey the bedding as I struggle to get out, as it has somehow wrapped itself all around me... it looks like there has-been some great fight during the night hours... or the greatest love... The body speaks...always asking for something.

Breakfast today was porridge with sultanas, a few walnuts for good measure, tinned prunes in natural juice and cinnamon.
Mmm.

A delight when eaten in the sunshine, in nature with the deafening sounds of the variety of birds and as I watch the rabbits come out of their burrow, there are two now...for they are multiplying. Lol and of course the pheasant returns in glorious colour. A little wash of sadness fleets over me, for one day I will leave here, not just this place... but this earth, for it is just so beautiful and I am so very blessed to be here. This opportunity I have had to experience it all in its entirety. Thank You. Thank You. Thank You for I really am so grateful.

I remember when my Nan passed away, for we were so very close, like the best of friends. I sat with my back against an oak tree in the park, as the wind gently blew... and I thought to myself you will not see this again or feel this breeze and I was sad not just for my children by then and me but for her because she truly was a loving soul.

We used to walk together quite a bit when I stayed with her weekends before I had a home of my own and then she would stay with me. Many rounds of Golf we played together in the park, with chats and laughs, so many times for she took us when mum could not and came to help me with the boys when mum could not too.

For mum was ill with Rheumatoid Arthritis and in a wheelchair and although she too was such a lovely woman, her life had gone in a different direction and had taken its toll. So she could not always do what Nan could but she would do things in a different way. Anyway, she could find to be with her grandchildren and us.

Love your elders all of them for they are only borrowed, their wisdom is great and we can learn so much from them, my Nan and mother were beautiful... for they both had hearts of gold...

If I can be half the person that you two were then I will be doing ok, I think to myself. I was with my mother when she passed and she said just before leaving...JESUS is standing in the room Tracy and I keep telling him to bugger off...

I laughed because my mum never swore and here she was telling off the greatest of men who had ever been born. Lol... She said I feel I need to stay longer for you all... but it appears to be impossible, (She was only in her 50's) for he returns over and over again, asking me to come... (Mum was not of any particular faith either, for she did not go to church but I know she prayed every day for her family in love and Jesus knew her heart).I knew in my heart too she had to go as she suffered so much but in my selfishness, I suppose I did not want it for I loved her so deeply. But as I knew the truth of life and I surely knew it then... I said, "It's okay mum, you do what you need to do, for you."

And with that, she was gone...

I loved you then and I love you now and that will never change, for what is truth always remains within the heart XX. This hair of mine is going to have to be shaved, it's a menace and I cannot be bothered with it anymore. It will change my whole appearance, as I am grey now underneath, age is a funny thing as time is an illusion... yet it does that somehow but who cares what others think!

For I know my heart and so does the Lord, so only care about what he thinks, as after all we are to be united one day in the great love. The eyes, I have always said are a gateway to the soul and they are bright, bright blue... beautiful inside and out that is what Swami said and I remembered this, "Never let anyone tell you...you are not beautiful."

Thank You Swami, as that really registered for I know who I am in my heart. Thank You. As I look in the mirror to comb my hair, I think again. It needs to come off for it is no longer a true representation of who I am, for the inside is not reflected on the outside. The pull of having my hair cut so short that it has almost gone has been coming back, each day in strength since being here. I have had it short before but not like this and I will be grey for the colour will leave with the cut.

I really do not know how much longer I can go on resisting the feeling shall I go into town or wait... just as I go to sit in meditation, a friend draws up and she says, "I don't know why but I have brought my hairdressing scissors." Omg, I say okay universe... It needs to come off... Now, are you ready she says, as once it's off that's it...just do it! I say like the NIKE advert...take action for it needs to be done. I am not vain about the hair I am more bothered about the colour. Lol.

As she starts to cut, she begins to wobble... are you sure? Are you sure she says? It's a bit late now I reply unless we have one half one way and one the other! The birds are in for a good night tonight as I can see it all falling to the floor... there appears to be more of it than I thought and as the feeling of the hair comes away it feels good somehow... liberating as if I have lost something.

As she brushes her hand over my head, she looks at me and says OMG... OMG Tracy, it really suits you but I hope to goodness you don't freak out. As I go in the shed and take the mirror, I smile for the inner now reflects the outer...I can see myself for the first time in a very long time! I shriek... .OMG and she screams in panic, so concerned that I hate it... as I come out smiling from ear to ear, she was holding her face so tightly.

I love it. I say just love I do not care what anyone else thinks, as for the first time I can see deep into my soul and it is beautiful! All afternoon she cannot stop staring as she repeats I cannot believe how much that suits you… It is you…and as I explain I can see Tracy now, she says yes but I have always seen you. Lol, I say, for we do not know how others see us until we see ourselves. Thank You for I am so grateful, not just for the haircut but for your love, care and support throughout this part of my journey… much gratitude always.

Another walk in the woods this time with such a feeling of freedom… it is quite unbelievable, the change that has occurred in such a short space of time and as I walk and contemplate my true nature.

I am filled with such warmth and love, for I could never have imagined myself being here at this place in my life, only a few years ago when I struggled to hand in my notice in the NHS. How things have moved on… so so much and I feel so blessed. There are many more stations, yet I am sure but as I look back on it all, how wonderful I think… for there have been so many already. I go back into meditation and a face flashes up from the past, a friend I have not seen for a while now in passing but not up close. What a difference now I think and laugh for not only the energy but the whole of my soul signature has changed… my vibration on this planet has certainly reached some sort of shift and he will be surprised when we meet.

He must be thinking over something as I know he is aware…but why today am I linking in? As I keep seeing him, standing there… thinking… as I cast my mind to the day of the week, I realise where he is and a vision enters… Oh, I see he is thinking of me. Never mind, one day you will see the truth and I believe that day is not too far away, as your book you lent me…I did wonder if you read it.

Such a wonderful day, how can things get better? But get better they do and I am so grateful Lord to you but I remember years ago you had said… Read… The Lord Is My Shepherd in the bible… I never really understood that message but now I do.

It's funny because the other day as I waited for a bus… my mind flew back to 2015 and the day I took a leap of faith. I was looking out of the window for I had shut myself away for 2 weeks, as I needed to make a decision. As I stood at the window, it felt like my soul jumped out of my body, for it frightened me… as I was on the third floor and for a moment… a split second, I thought I had fallen. But as I heard the leap of faith I realised the soul was calling me into action. I went for a walk that day, just the same as yesterday and as I walked past a field, very similar to then, the sheep stopped still… motionless and then walked altogether over to join me at the fence.

Do you think I have food I say, as this is almost a repeat performance of 2015… for as they stand and stare, it's like they are waiting for me to speak as they do not chew but just stand frozen? The chicken appears… no this can't be right where was that hiding? As exactly what occurred before… then not just one but two and then three, as I get a little spooked and think… omg… this cannot be happening… and that was before I had my hair cut. Lol…So maybe do not think Tracy, for the mind is not the control, let go and just be…be whoever you were born to be… remember that and you will be okay!

Well, I am pretty tired now as it has been an eventful day and as I last gazed across the hills at the sunset… my heart was overflowing… for the sight is so sweet, so like the nectar of the honey… and as a kestrel flies out of the tree, how blessed am I…

how blessed to be here, in the here and now, as it hits my heart again with a thud.

The sun has been warm today as it appeared to sink through my jeans and each day as I sit outside for longer and longer, I relish the day… I will stay out for hours under the stars with a friend. For right now I am still a little nervous, as alone in the wood but one day that will not be the case… for someone will have joined me, a special soul and I don't mean GOD… for they are here already… in my heart.

One day I am going to the observatory with friends in Kielder, so that will be nice too…for I have never been and I know that will be magical… for the stars light up the dark sky and I love them. As a child, I used to watch them all the time and one Xmas when I had a family of my own, I bought a telescope for my son; as he loved them too.

Shame we lost that somewhere in the moves… my binoculars as well to see the birds… I suddenly remember the message, where are they, I did not find them at the weekend? And my camera… for I was a keen photographer as a teenager, funny how things get passed down, as my son went into the creative field and then settled in a career in film… did I ever say my son, how proud I am of you.

News of a theatre group has reached me… An outdoor theatre group is booked to come to the Garden Station for I cannot wait… Midsummer Night's Dream… Ahh… amazing… my white wicker picnic basket will have to come out for that, as a beautiful gift from my daughter one Xmas. For I am the queen of picnics. Lol… a picnic and theatre, in the outdoors what a delight!

Maybe it does get better all the time until we are in heaven… heaven on earth.

Good Night and God Bless for may the God-ness of the day be with you. As the universe is a friend.

Always X.

DAY 17

Good Morning and God Bless for may the God-ness of the day be with you. As the universe is a friend.

The Dawn Chorus woke me but I decided to lay in today for nourishment is needed. I have had a disturbed night of many dreams… as many aspects leave me ready for the new beginnings.

Dreams of my sister… .our richness, of our relationship and of our surroundings but a noticing of how still the trivial can interlude… I can see how I can live anywhere in poverty or riches, as it appears not to bother me anymore. As the more, I have let go of the material world for the inner, in recognition of the truth of the only true love. The revolving motion of the universe as it always expands… from within into the outer space, as it seeks to expand over and over into the nothingness for it is constant. I see a friend in my dream, someone that I have met before in dream state yet not in the earthly world… for they are in their process of unraveling and choose to enter other places. Funny how souls come in… in different ways, to meet with you and acknowledge your growth. For they had in the dream, the opportunity to come with me but they chose not…they chose other pleasures, other places of illusion and not the riches of the greatest of all creation on earth. As I eat my breakfast today, I am feeling a little emotional like a huge shift has taken place, my eyes are misty again and yet the significance of such a shift I am not certain yet. The feeling is it is still bigger than I can possibly imagine, for it is not yet fully manifested.

I relax and trust in all… I can do, just one step at a time but this feeling does not leave me, so I decide to meditate. Throughout the meditation tears flow in the release of something and a more significant space emerges in my field of understanding, as it is still growing.

I can feel its expansion and as I allow the energy to pass to me through and from me... I do wonder for a second, where this will all end. But that is not mine to know, for it is God's alone. As I walk the woods in the beautiful sunshine... I sit for a while and link into nature. The birds, the trees, the flowers, the insects, the toads... all that come within my sight and space and I feel at one with them all as I watch a Buzzard, as it soars out of the tops of the pines. I stop for a moment to gaze down at a toad, who is looking for a mate. I laugh for we as humans are much the same, yet worlds apart.

The toad is small in regards to the land of the giants... yet we are probably not any more wise, for he could have the brains of any man. For who are we to judge in the grander scheme of things. As I walk on further, I see another that has surely died, for he has withered away and turned jet black, as the insects now take their food from him. For everything physical stays on earth... one day in dust we too will fall away, as the physical does not leave, only the 'Grace' of the heart. This merges... into the light to become at one again, with our creator and the greatest love. As the day progresses, I am left with an unsettled feeling of something not being quite right and as I listen to my inner intuition, I feel I need to make a call.

To ring my daughter for something has happened... I go back into the shed and pull a card, it is parenting so I know I need to speak with her, as she would not disturb me in any way as she never asks for help. So I put my phone on for a few minutes, out of the silence and link back into the world. As she answers, I ask if all is okay and she says yes... but my intuition is telling me it is not, so I enquire further. It is then she tells me the truth. As she starts to speak, she must have realised because she said, "You know though… don't you" Yes, I say I was told yesterday… and I had a vision of your dad in place that I did not recognise nearby for he has not left. She then went on to tell me what had occurred and I was able to reassure her that what she is doing is right. The right thing for her and no one else matters, not him or me or her sister but what is best for herself.

She struggles to let go… because she cares… and I know this feeling well, for I have held on to things myself before, for far too long. She voices something and I say 'Well done Alice' for in your realisation… you have grown and all is meant to be exactly as it is right now. How much you have changed in such a short space of time and I am so very proud of you. I say that when my book is finished, I shall give her a copy, for she needs to read it through. She hears me…I know, for I can feel it in her heart and she is beginning to learn to trust.

We laugh as I tell her about my hair and that it is virtually no more… OMG, she says… as I say do not worry for it suits me, I look like a Buddhist… and with that, she laughs some more. I love you I say so very much and no matter where I go…I may be on my spiritual path but I will never leave you, for you are always in my heart. She understands and now sees… I'm sure the truth of everything and then as she speaks, I am blessed with her love, so I say goodbye for now and switch off. Another walk around the woods and I meet with a few people along the way, two women having a chat and two fishermen. Then as I come out of the deeper part of the wood, I stumble across an elderly man who is a bit shocked to see me… for I say hello… good afternoon and he continues to stare in bewilderment.

For in his head, he cannot understand. I can see it all running through his mind and I'm laughing to myself, for we all judge on appearances... as he tries to weigh me up by looking me up and down, he's just not sure what to think and what I represent, as anyway I just appeared... out of the depths of the wood. I walk further down a track across a field and then beyond it all, into the stillness of the wild... as I sit on a log and survey the scene, it is so stunning... the green fields like carpets of rolling hills. And it reminds me of the view of the earth from a plane...

England I love it here still... in the warmer weather mind... the winters maybe I will leave but for now, I will remain. As I sit and link into nature for about ten minutes in. I suddenly feel the presence of someone. I cannot see them anywhere but I know that they are somewhere near and as I listen further still within, they suddenly appear. At the end of the field is a little gate and they walk through, a man whose face I cannot see in the distance... friend or foe I say to myself but I don't really know. So I decide to leave for now as I am in the wild and as I wait and stand and think. How is my head in relation to my body, for I need to walk swiftly and with ease? With that, a noticing occurs as my arms are slightly outside of my body, so I relax my muscles and let them hang, just as the skeleton is designed to support itself.

With that, I think about my knees and bend them slightly, for I need to move and I need to move now... My training has come in well with the FM Alexander Technique, for before I know it, I am moving with the grace of a gazelle... Across the fields and down the track and over the crossroads I go, for now, I know these woods so well. I do not turn to look behind for if he ran, he could catch me but I do not want to give out any energy like fear, so I continue on in the Alexander way. In what seems like minutes which usually takes half an hour, I arrive at my destination and make myself a cuppa. It is incredible how my intuition has heightened during my time here, for connecting to nature and being silent, has opened me up even further.

What a beautiful day as I work outside and get ready for work tomorrow, my itinerary for the day is ready as I am holding a Wellness Workshop at the Garden Station. I have included my talk "We are not our story" For I want to start at the beginning and then move forward... The red root chakra, the labyrinth and the Earth Breath meditation and sounds... all beneficial for grounding and connecting oneself to the inner garden of love.

I help to raise awareness and allow others to see their way, as they too begin to weed their inner space and plant good seeds. I am really looking forward to the fun that we shall share... and also the first Drum Circle on Sunday, as we will sing and clap and play the instruments in front of the campfire, together as friends in camaraderie and love... so many creative days we can share here.

The seashore is another destination for me with people in tow, for workshops abroad and so much fun to be experienced. The friends I've made here and the places we have talked about, maybe Portugal... maybe Malta definitely Assisi still, India yes and more for I have six months to fill. A trip is planned to a monastery in Manchester in May and an overnight stay... I am so pleased now that my car broke down and I was forced to stay.

For the Lord and the universe had other plans for me... and although I know I will return to Essex one day, for now, I need to be here... and I am happy to accept. I already have bookings for Essex waiting, as recommendations came through, so a short trip back down south will be good too. Let's have an adventure...why not! I also say the highlands and the islands are calling, and another hermitage here deeper in the woods maybe so, and so many openings... best not to think but just to allow the flow.

A wonderful dinner was eaten tonight... I must be dreaming, for everything is becoming real, so real. And as my friend calls in so quick that she lost her father the other day, I give her the biggest of hugs and a kiss and tell her to call by. Reiki is needed at this time and I can certainly provide it. A GIFT for her with all heart and all my love always. The stars are out, the owl is hooting and I am ready for bed... another lovely day was had today and I am filled with gratitude.

Good Night and God Bless for may the God-ness of the day be with you. As the universe is a friend.

Always X

DAY 18

Good Morning and God Bless for may the God-ness of the day be with you. As the universe is a friend.

Dawn Chorus… I am getting used to this now. Lol… as the sleep has rested the physical and now I am ready for work. As I go to sit in meditation, I am told to start off with my drum… as I like to be prepared and in an as positive energy field as I can for when the people arrive. As I listen to the beat and go within for a few minutes, a small prayer comes back that was given in a previous meditation, so I write it here…

Mother Earth and Father Sky.
Bless this world and all that cry.
Release us from Illusions spell…
As Angels Above and Guardians Below…
Grant us Joy and Love inflow.
Go with Grace and Peace and Love.
As within. As without.
As above. As below.
So be it so!
OM……………… X 3

I am ready, ready for the day to unfold in love and joy and understanding, for we are all as one, seeking the same place of happiness. Yet we look in the wrong places, we turn over so many stones in our search and all along it was there yet hidden from our sight.

But today we shall start the journey together within… to find yourself so you too can return to the Promised Land, the richest of all. Do not give up they say, just before the MIRACLE occurs… As I have qualified as a Reiki Master Teacher, I have used the GRACE symbol more and more as Grace within the heart is such a beautiful energy and as I speak of it in my talks, the 5th secret chamber of Grace. This reminds me of the saying by Simon Treselyan, as he is slightly different from that of the Taoist Grace symbol but one that I use often and love, as he is in my lineage. He 'heard' like me in meditation and I believe this to be true, for he was using his God-given gifts to bring it through for you.

He said in intuition the following statement, more detailed than mine but I too use this in my Reiki self-healing sessions with others, for it was given by source and as I have been initiated into the spiritual lineage of Mikao Usui, he channeled…

Let all being throughout all time.
Throughout all space.
Throughout all dimensions.
And planes of existence, and non-existence.
Be forever liberated, from all suffering.
And fully experience eternal joy.
Of supreme liberation.
NOW fully manifest……

I do not believe in coincidence and the information does arrive in many ways but we have to see it, find it, feel it within our heart, embody it and then take action upon it when shown. Well, we are tired but happy at the end of the day, the first in the line of workshops to be held here in the Garden Station, my magical place of love. Each person including myself are having their own personal shifts throughout the day. For whatever is required is usually felt and people are beginning to embrace themselves. I am so pleased to be a part of this, for it is very rewarding to watch the signs and the signals of change, not just for others but myself too, for each and every person teaches me something new. I always remember that we are both the student and the teacher.

As a lady leaves, she says something quite profound... of which I am aware... I am not quite their... yet, Lol... but thank you, for I know it was meant from the heart, as a compliment, so I accept in love, as it was given. I always say no matter how many people there are present in a meeting, it is a gift, as the right people are still in the right place at the right time and for the right reasons... so thank you, I am so grateful.

We have completed many things today, a mindful walk, meditations, drum work and education, along with my talk. The energy has altered over the hours that we have spent together and a change has occurred somehow, plus relaxed faces are now before me, as they leave... so pleasing to see the smiles and to have the hugs and goodbye, for today was a lovely day at work. I love my job... and I will never leave this path... for I have found the calling of my authentic self.

As I walk through the woods for the final time today before sleep, I am feeling the energy of the trees supporting me, nourishing me and replenishing my soul, for it has been busy but as I contemplate, I know it is surely just the beginning of something very special indeed.

Good Night and God Bless for may the God-ness of the day be with you. As the universe is a friend.

Always X

DAY 19

Good Morning and God Bless for may the God-ness of the day be with you. As the universe is a friend.

A very mixed up night for me again last night, as the outside world re-enters my field, it is funny how it affects me now, as the periods of silence has done something. The world is a hectic place even when it is not that busy in people, as it is the energy of the mind that is rushing around everywhere in the consciousness.

We are still processing yesterday as it was such a lovely day, a WORKSHOP here at the Garden Station and transformation has occurred, for us all in one way or another even if it is not yet fully manifested, for everyone was tired... a SHIFT has taken place.

The owners of The Garden Station both saw... not with their physical eyes but with vision... the Garden Station in a different way... and I saw that vision too last month, so confirmation for me as I hear them say. The Lord does work in mysterious ways but I am pleased for them as they deserve it...for their kindness abounds and they are special to this world. We have to see it first and THEN believe it... then the energy will drop to the earth, so we should all watch what we are thinking.

I know this... for when in Assisi I was so concerned for my group on an outing that I kept thinking about health and safety. How to ensure they were safe and avoid any accidents. For even though we could access help, I felt responsible.

As we all visited a little chapel before the sacred art circles and go to pray, as I get up to leave, I hit my head so hard on a concrete archway, that the 'CRACK' is heard… Yet not a mark was on my forehead and how I never fainted? Was for sure a miracle…Lol, that will teach you Tracy, I said to myself, be careful what you think about!

A family has been in for Mothers Day Tea and how I remember those days, for three small children in tow and virtually the same age gap as mine were.

Enjoy it, I think to myself for in the blink of an eye it will be gone, as they are only lent and they grow from the baby to the adult in what appears to be a second. As the dad throws the little one over his shoulder for she will not stay still… so full of energy… all she wants to do is explore this world it all in its glory for she is truly beautiful. Her energy is oozing from her, as she runs up to me and just looks… .I love children for they are so happy… Don't grow up not in your heart anyway… remember it's a trap!

The dog has joined me for an afternoon nap in the warm while I write and I should really get my wellingtons on and go for a walk but the warmth of this shed and the love here is a draw… maybe in a minute for I have plenty of time. The clocks went forward, did they not? I forgot! As I went around today even more confused than ever… Lol.

This world is definitely crackers… just live by natures rules, as far as we can, as the greatest of pleasure is here and NOW. Woody is up and knocking hard on that tree and the birds are singing… wonder what type of day today will bring. As I go in and out of the world today, I see some happiness for it is Mothers Day, so families are out enjoying their time together and others in concern for either they have lost a mother or their mother is not well… So hard when people suffer especially the young for they are bewildered and not sure of life and how it should be as some do not yet have wisdom on their side or they could be having to hold the parenting role.

So I bless these even more today, for they need our prayers, love and support along their way. Even if they do not say, try to see the bigger plan for them and you, for it may be they are to teach us… something today. As the day progresses and a walk is finally had, the trees, the energy, it rises again like the sap, it appears to flow as I cannot wait to write for The 'One' Road has just been birthed and fills me with delight.

The delight for God and all that reigns, the secret world of Love for the 21 basic principles are here… for the living. I cannot wait to share these, for they are truly special yet common sense it appears… so why? Why are we all missing the road so frequently? Free will again, I feel… A lovely day all around and a time for reflection as I read the principles back to myself. How far you have travelled Tracy in just two years… the changes are so stark to see and feel… unbelievable really, yet not… for I have worked hard with sweat and tears and I can see the path I trod along the way, as only with hindsight could I truly see this.

The steps were there and given… all I did was follow in trust and love and faith and hope that there was something much bigger than me. Anything that I do now is not mine, for I am only the conduit… I feel blessed however that somehow and I am not sure why but I was given these gifts to share with all.

One glorious day, I hope I can return and speak with the Lord. I truly want to thank them for every single day of my life for everything, as it has shaped me and helped me so much along the way.

Thank you. Thank You. Thank you will never be enough, so I will keep you in my heart and spread the word of Love. Always... as the evening draws and people arrive for the Drum Circle, I can see a sad face for only 3... Do you remember 3 tell one and turn to 6?

The right people are in the right place at the right time for the right reasons... always. As we begin and the energy starts to build I see a change as they begin to drink the water from the fountain of life... the puzzled faces, the disbelief, the smiles, the shouts of joy... my god this can't be happening they say, IS THIS REAL? As I laugh for, I KNOW the truth. We have a break, for they need to rest, as sudden 'joy' is seen and all ask for water... Lol, not tea. Then we progress... it is like a stream as we flow together and dance within the heart, for it is born... the planting of the good seed and the growth is already sprouting forth. As I love to watch their faces like children in the best of time...as we sing and hear, and see... and hear the chant... and drum and rattle and shake the tambourine, with all our might.

I see the hit... as it hits hard... straight into the heart, like cupids arrow as it reaches its spot... better than any football match... as I want to shout from the rooftops... GOAL!!

I look into the eyes that have changed... for they have truly seen and as bewilderment now leaves, in trust... they FEEL the unconditional love. With smiles of joy and hugs so tight, I see the tears flow... for they have truly loved tonight, and now they KNOW.

Was it magical? Maybe but only of God's Love, for in goodness only, everything grows as it should. The Owl is hooting and people leave so differently from before, as they now want to run... and tell all of their experience... and spread the news. I gaze at the stars so bright tonight and go to rest, to meditate and say my prayers of thanks, for it has been yet another wonderful day, and I am so grateful.

Good Night and God Bless for may the God-ness of the day be with you. As the universe is a friend. Always

During the night, I am awoken quickly... as spirit make sure I know, as I feel a snare and have to shake my leg, for someone is afraid... afraid I may succeed where they have yet... not... why do this to yourself and me, I think? For it makes me feel so sad, for God's love is here for us all to share together and there is so much fun to be had.

Yet you try to use your magic against me... but it will not work, for I am working in the light and will always be shown the dark... it burns and pricks me like thorns trying to dig and dig to hold me tight but it will not be allowed... can you not see? For I can fly free... and WILL.

The Eagle is not ensnared for they are free to fly as they were born to be and now I am free... free to be me... my authentic self, so leave me well alone as I cast you out. Use your magic if you will and turn it on yourself, to use it for your greatest good and help yourself within. For God is good and created... creation itself... so Goodness only in your magic please for healing yourself and all that come before you. If you want to come, then come but come in PEACE for anything else will be known and seen.

It soon gives up and drifts away… as I send a prayer of light, God helps these people in your love and love them all tonight.

Good Night Sweet Dreams and plant the good seeds.

Always. X

DAY 20

Good Morning

The day has started well as usual but I am a little anxious I have to say, as I have to go into town for provisions today and to see my son. For it is his birthday tomorrow... 35, where have the years gone? And to see my 2-year-old granddaughter, as she needs to desensitise herself to my new look!

As I reach the town, the business of the place takes over immediately, so much so that I have decided to continue with my silence for a few extra days. To make up for these lost days, when I have to come into the world and to also ease myself back into the suffering, when I am at the barn for 2 weeks straight after. As re-entry is going to be difficult, I know that now but I will do it and do it well, as I have completed intensives before and seen it then but I suppose not to this degree.

My mind is still confused for it likes to know itself how it has known itself to be as all these changes are immense, especially the pace of it so far. As the last two years have been the most intense of all. On arrival, I speak with voice before she can see... as seeing me will be a shock for her. My son smiles as he can see her face but I cannot for she is around the corner hidden... and as I turn towards the corner too, I see it on her face as she shrinks back in surprise. So I carry on speaking the normal way I do, to her in love and she smiles for she sees me with her heart and not her eyes. When I reach her she allows me the cuddle that I have been so looking forward to. For she is one of my delights of every day, I love her as much as I do all of you.

Upon leaving, I place a card on the mantle shelf for my first born son as he is now a parent too and I can see myself reflected in him, for we are after all what we know. The good mainly he has copied but I can see other older traits of mine too, I'm hoping that he will realise himself, as he grows through the illusion.

For his daughter one day is bound to say... You do not understand... or I hate you! Lol, for as parents we try our best... to no avail because they always believe the rest. It is funny now as I sit and watch all that they do; it is like watching a film of times before when I was parenting you. One day when we shall sit together... from above and watch this back and we shall have the biggest laugh together for you will say... You twat!

I can hear it now ringing forth in my ears... such fun to be had. The day is soon consumed by life... so this recording will be short, for on my return I have done nothing but cry... real tears of love. Love for you all, as I really do... but this is my time now and I have to see it through.

For I was born to live a life just the same as you and all that I wanted for you then... I still do, your dreams and so much more. But if I give up and come back now... it will have been to waste, so I cannot but I will go first and I will set the pace. The leader in me yet you cannot see, for it is still not there for you... but one day the shock of it, will suddenly appear and hit... hit you in the heart.

For it will manifest itself in front of you... and you will think what the heck? But it will have been present for a while, yet not seen through your eyes. For as the changes were occurring you chose your own free will and you were enjoying yourself, as you went along in life in your own sweet merry way, learning your own lessons and making your own mistakes throughout each day. For we all do it… we are human… and what else is there but to learn, until one day a gate will open and then we shall all return in Love.

Rules are man-made. But Loving and Caring for each other unconditionally should be the norm. As the tears flow I see a vision, the second one today of you my friend… One this morning as you arose and as I watch your face, no smiles were there on this very morning, when you awoke. Then tonight I see you again and I see and feel a decision has been made, for you have realised something and you are no longer afraid…

I watch as the scene unfolds and I BELIEVE… for I can feel it, not just see it…so I shall wait for the day when this comes, and as I will welcome you as I always have in unconditional love.

I need to rest, as my body speaks, for it has taken its toll on me today and as the warm and comfy bed is ready, I need to sink and be within its covers. Tomorrow I am back in complete silence and I will be nourishing me and only me, for it is my priority… now… for I love you, Tracy.

Thank you for I have enjoyed it still, as everything is precious… always.

Good Night and God Bless…in goodness for the God-ness of the day will stay with you. As the universe is a friend.

Always X

DAY 21

Good Morning and may the God-ness of the day be with you. For the universe is a friend.

The day has started, but my body will not play the game as it does not want to move, so I turn over and drift. The sun has not come out yet and it feels cold... April 2nd, yet still cold air as frost appears and sometimes hail... for the season of the sun in bloom is not yet upon us. The birds are chirping though for they do not care as long as they have seed, so I get up to feed... A little blue tit comes to the bench just outside my window, as I have placed the St Francis hands in sight so I can watch him closely. His colours and delicate features I love and the sound of his chirp as he rejoices at his find this morning, for he is so grateful.

The other two tables soon fill and the pheasant arrives, I have not seen the rabbits for a few days. The owner did tell of the deer at the weekend three of them but I have missed them again, for they arrive early and nose around the wood. One day perhaps before I leave, I will see them before they see me and run away into the denser bracken.

Fear has been arising again... every time I go into the world, it appears to try and trick me into staying in the old ways. It seems I am trapped? Can I travel still? Will I be able to move? Are my dreams to be fulfilled? Good Lord, how can it affect me so quickly after only a day, outside? Swami did say do not buy into it Tracy, just remember it is all in the consciousness... so I kick it out... and tell it to leave. As I open the book to study, a little piece of the information jumps out... Ask, and ye will receive... I read it over a few times and realise it is saying that if I truly believe and ask in the father's name, I can have anything that I so desire.

I know this to be true... so I change a few affirmations around, to ensure the intentions are full of goodness, clear, ready for the new moon as I need to be clear...with everything. As they are already manifesting and I need to be sure that this is definitely what I want.

As I read further, synchronicity occurs as it says about 40 nights in the wilderness... then Jesus was sure who he was... his product... he was clear and then able to stay true to himself. I can see the resemblance, for each day I do become clearer... as I continue to check in and "Know Thyself Well."

After breakfast, I go for a walk and feel the energy of the trees again, I wonder why I have not always felt them so strongly before. As I stand with my back to a very large oak and let it soak right into me, as I merge with its energy and it fills me to the brim with love. A steady stream of relaxing waves flows, as it fills my every crevice of the trunk of the physical from the soles of the feet to the tip of my head. For some reason, I think about Sandringham in Norfolk and the environment.

The trees and the gardens there, that I have walked amongst them many times and with the Royals, all their good work around the world, for they do try to help where they can, to raise awareness and the standards of lives in other countries and this. I am not a royalist but I do watch with interest at times, for they are learning too... their lessons as we all are, so I do not judge. As I speak of hail it starts again... and my little shed, my home is rather full of holes, so I maybe need to start again with the paper mâché.

The more I fill, the more I seem to find... by the time I have mended this house it will be fit for a Queen. Lol... I have been in silence for hours now, as the noises appear so loud, every crack and bang I can hear from miles around. I go for a nap this afternoon and I am awoken with such a fright for it is a deafening sound of what? Is it overhead? Is it a plane about to crash land upon my shed? It sounds so low I nearly panic and run... it reminds me of war and air raid shelters, not that I ever knew. But the fear they must have felt and now in war-torn countries... families all scared for their lives.

I cannot open the door to see above, for I have locked it and in my fear, I cannot see the key, it is so so loud. Bombs could drop... or the shed could fall over on top of me, for it must be close as the land appears to vibrate. I know a similar sound from army bases as I have lived near, when their jets have taken off from standing... straight up into the air and it is like supersonic sound to the ears but as I listen it appears in my mind that these are army helicopters.

My heart is thudding and I think again of the children who are in the war zones, having lost their homes and parents too at times, displaced and alone. How hard it must be for them, where is humanity? Where have we gone, for goodness sake, wake up and care about each and every one? For these are someone's father, mother, child and friend, do not harm another... please I pray for it may come the day, that it is you. I look outside and the ground has turned white for the hail has joined like dots... covering the ground like snow, it is coming down so hard, it is amazing to watch from the wood, as the bird feeder is now covered in little white pellets along with everything else.

How weird...this weather... is it climate change again? As it crosses my mind and I think what a mess we are placing ourselves in. I pull on my dressing gown with a hood for it has suddenly gone bitter... but at least I am blessed to have a roof for now. The helicopters have gone but I can hear them still, far away in the distance... I wonder why they came down so low... The bird is shouting now for he cannot reach his seed, for the snow pellets... I shall have to go outside and sort it out for him. As the sun breaks through, I go for a walk and it is truly beautiful.

I hear the birds but do not see much, as we are disturbed again by the growing sound of the helicopters. They are coming back this way and I can hear but not yet see, then suddenly they appear from above the wood, flying quite low to the ground, two of them, but suddenly no sound... for they must have landed somewhere close in a field. I decide to walk back because I do not want to come across any soldiers, for they will get a surprise to see me in the middle of no man's land.

I have relaxed and nourished myself all day, eaten good food, studied, walked and prayed, meditations were good and I saw my shed like a temple... take off your shoes they say, so I do as I light a candle and speak again to the father. They see what is going on I know... as I say with a smile... am I there yet? The light is dull as the hail has brought the clouds and as it begins to darken, I decide the best place tonight for me is back to bed, for I am still tired... tired of any thoughts, any at all as all just want to give up... surrender to the Lord. I am going to try my absolute best tonight to let go of every muscle that I possess in this physical body, including my mind... as I am sure it is blind... I need the Lord to take over now and guide me all the way home, for he can be the driver... as I have had enough.

What was that saying I heard once, as it flashes through…Ah yes, Let go and let God! Sounds easy… Lol, but not… for it is the hardest of all to achieve. I am not usually one to give up with anything, so it appears peculiar almost back to front… for giving up is ALL that's needed. My body aches, my mind… is tired… and the waves appear, for they swirl and twirl internally, they know the truth. For goodness sake, Tracy… Stop it! Let go it screams… I can hear it in my heart and feel it too, so I breathe…slowly in and out and…

Good Night and God Bless for I can hardly write, for they are calling me tonight… May the God-ness of the day stay with you. For the universe is a friend.

Always X

DAY 22

Good Morning and God Bless for may the God-Ness of the day be with you. As the universe is a friend.

The 3rd of April... Well, Day 22 over halfway through and as I open my eyes, I cannot hear the birds, I must have missed Dawn Chorus. But as it is so cold, I can feel it through the holes, the draft as it billows through in the shed and I snuggle down under my three quilts! 3 for day 3 of April I think to myself, a special number and how blessed am I because the homeless are so very, very cold...

Eventually, I rise from the pit of warmth, as the shed is creaking, and I wonder why. I hope it lasts out the rest of my time here I think... but Tracy is careful what you think about. I slept last night with a special crystal under my pillow and had many dreams, some of which I remember. The St Francis purse that I bought from the monastery in Assisi holds it for me. As I bought one for me and one for my friend, so they too could have assistance at all times. I shall review the dreams later for there were a few of significance... As I open the light curtain that I hung to the window... OMG... OMG... OMG... I laugh now! For in the night, snow has laid like a beautiful white carpet, it has covered everything... no wonder the shed is creaking!!!

With the excitement of a child, I want to run outside... but with the hesitancy of an adult so funny for my Nan's words of caution in her love ring... and I think about layers, boots and all that I need... Lol!!

The freshness in the air, no flowers to be seen, the birds are quiet, confused...what has happened? One minute spring, next back to winter, although I do remember seasons years ago as a child, when in May on my birthday we had snow, for I was worried that none of my friends would get through to my party. Well, I shall have a party today for sure… it is not my birthday yet but it feels like it in my heart… as I enjoy the moment. For the land is so beautiful a 'picture' of sheer delight so much so that I want to photograph it? I lost a glove yesterday, so now with only one, I keep one hand in the pocket whilst the other is warm in the glove holding onto my walking stick.

That is the plan… and layers…yes Nan. REMINDER…the homeless need gloves and so much more… It is coming down heavy… and does not look like it will stop, so maybe we are in for a long haul. I pulled a card last night and it said 'Time Out'… they always know before me… I thought I had time out, THIS 40 DAYS, but this could be real, as there will be no work for me this weekend if it settles. Hot chocolate in front of the fire and lovely food, what more do I need today… nothing. Today I rest but on the 40th day, as I emerge, I am going to start contacting centres, to see if there is anything that I can do for them.

My skills include that of a City and Guilds Trained Hairdresser for over twenty years so I can cut hair. Previously a social worker in Drug and Alcohol Services Mental Health Learning Disabilities and Palliative care… I know some things… for I have seen many. Previously cleaner… when necessary I have cleaned many places for I am not afraid of hard work and will do as required. Also, my time was spent… for many years as a caregiver and a parent and a foster parent - the hardest jobs of all, believe me…

Businesses of my own, a Ballroom and Latin American dancer competing for many years travelling around the country, working hard, long hours until late at night, 7 nights a week plus going to work and a Sunday competing all day, complementary therapy, cook and bottle washer and house sitting / dog sitter... plus now... Professional speaker motivating people, showing them through my eyes and my life that... "We are not our story" and Spiritual guide, the... Inner Guru Propagator enabling people to find themselves again within... what else is there?

Perhaps I was meant to be all round 'whole' so that my skills could be shared where needed. As all are at different stations and need different things at different times of their lives, for everyone is unique. Like a garden needs many tools, to weed and complete the job, cultivate and grow, from the seedling to the plant... the most beautiful flower of all. The 'Rose' in bloom.

The homeless need gloves... and warmth, both outer and inner as it keeps returning to my mind today, for I am concerned for them in love. I can see the bigger picture and more... for I am blessed with vision and Gods Love in my heart and I will spread the Unconditional Love I promise, everywhere I travel. For it is not always spoken but it is felt in the heart... BOOM - Like an explosion of Love. So be it so...

After my walk in the wood, I decided to study and I CRY out from the heart, for such a selfish fool am I. As I study St Clare, her life growing up and her mother with their devout love for the people, doing what they could. I fall to my knees in such remorse...and prayer for I AM TRULY SORRY. OMG, what an idiot I have been, for I have been in so much lack... that I was blind... to the truth of how wealthy I really was. Charity boxes, pennies I placed in them... such shame I feel and so many needed help or the money could have multiplied so many times.

Where was I? What was I thinking? Oh God, please forgive me. £300 was probably the most I gave of late, a mere pittance, in comparison to what I had, what a waste. I spent on myself, friends and the family in selfish ways… and did not learn my lesson. Thank God that I did not win the 4 million winnings at the time, for I have not been worthy. I thank God the ticket was not placed on… as it should have been, as we would have won that day, no winners it said when I checked but that would have been us as it was my numbers. Please forgive me… I say again and again, between my sobs, for now I see the truth and I will not be such a fool again for now, I KNOW.

We do not need to hoard, or be selfish to our own ends, for balance in the love of the Lord is always given, when we truly see. I cannot express in words how much my heart is breaking… for I am a wretch for sure… I even placed a soft throw on the floor to pray, for goodness sake Tracy… you pampered princess… give yourself a slap, for you should know better than that. I will have to work hard on forgiveness today for that I surely need, and to forgive myself… The 'One' Road Principle 21 Forgiveness, For they know not what they do, including thyself.

As I mull over it again… I cannot change the past and the future has not yet arrived, for one thing for sure I KNOW, this anyway in the present. Today has been such a day of learning on a very deep level, always the student and the teacher and my dreams make even more sense now and it is only 11.30. As I glance at my watch that adorns my wrist. A £200 gold watch did I need it? It tells the time, the rules made by man, any watch would have done the job, with a clock face on. This 40 days… I realise it is to clear all that was left within, in fear… for I need to be completely clear… to KNOW which way to go.

I will follow the steps, I promise Lord… if you allow me to continue in your name in service after today… for I have been an idiot, you must have shaken your head and thought… Duh… not again!!!

The more I read today, the harder it hits for I can see my calling so many years ago as a child, as I used to stare out of the window at home and knew there was more to life than this. I used to think about becoming a nun but we were not Catholic, anyway by then, I had discovered boys and they appeared much more interesting.

My life was busy between school and then college and work, as the outside world takes over. Yet as a child, I knew that something had to be shared… a love like no other. For I used to walk the streets with all of the neighbours' children, the babies I would take them out to give their mothers some rest and picnics were had across the park as I COLLECTED THEM all and took them with me. Jam sandwiches, sausage rolls, lemonade, and a bag of crisps. LOL… a great time. A child with cerebral palsy, his mother loved him so much and so did I, for he was such a beautiful boy with shining eyes and full of smiles.

I used to love to take him out in his pram and as I think back, I was probably 9 or 10 but the love I felt, for all of them were like family. As I grew I so wanted to be a social worker but at the age of 16 being so shy, I was persuaded by my parents not to go down that road.

You are too sensitive they said, you will not cope so be a hairdresser instead, for you will never be out of work for hair always grows. I did as I was told and followed their path, which I did enjoy… in my creativity, for I could see how a person's hair should be as it framed their face. It brought me out of my shell, as everyone told me their problems and again, the calling came to be in service. So I changed my plan in older age and returned to education, where I learnt how to be the social worker. I learnt to drive, as this was a necessity and empowered myself at the same time to become a better version of me.

I loved my job, for I loved the people with all my heart and as I worked alongside the families, it was such a special time, for they became like family in my heart. My boss would call me sticky fingers for I could not go anywhere, without coming back with a new case. Please, I would say they need our help! OK… would be the reply with a sigh and I would smile in thanks, for I loved them and I loved them all, even amongst the angst…

It was hard at times, for man-made rules and professional boundaries were laid, for I was not a friend at all but there to do a job and resources were often not what I could get for them. If they had been my own, for sure everything they would have been given, for having been a mother, a wife, a parent and a caretaker myself for I knew their pain… for I sat in their shoes and their hearts. I had been working all along following my calling, yet still, I did not see, for I was truly blind… I used to pray and say when Lord? Can I be of service? For you see I truly am an idiot, so how can others follow me… for if I don't know who I am or where I am going, so Clarity is needed… to be clear who I AM. These 40 days have helped a lot to confirm so much for me, for I have felt it brewing and brewing within. Especially these last two years.

For my world has turned itself upside down… just like the Magic Faraway Tree. Tracy has morphed into… a product of 'Love' on The 'One' Road and will share this now for she believes in Love, herself and finally… 'KNOWS HERSELF WELL'. If mistakes are made I apologise and try not repeat, for there is no better time than now, to be unique, my imprint as I came to this earth to be… Our authentic self as it rises… from the very depths, like the Phoenix as it rises out of the ashes… Transformation in love and light and with so many blessings, for we are truly blessed. I want to jump for joy again…for this road is truly beautiful, once you accept its ups and downs, in learning, in truth and honesty, as we look in the mirror and say I Love You for we are all loved by God and we can see this reflected in us, through the eyes, for the eyes are a gateway to the soul.

I have always loved my eyes, even from a young child, I used to look in the mirror at them, for they were so bright and blue… how I loved them and now… finally I know what I was truly seeing. My SOUL signature reflected through the Love in the heart of God and back to me in the mirror… .Thank you for I am so grateful. Another walk is had and the birds fed, for the snow is beginning to melt now, with the sun… The deer prints are melting away back to earth, so that man cannot follow them, so I meditate for a while, feeling the waves as they wash and build in the flow within and then rest. I keep being shown various things as confirmation that all is well and the right timing is near, for I am shown progress.

The birds feed again hungrily and sing too for they are happy again… the owner pops by to check in and make sure I am safe, so as a thank you, I decided to do an impromptu sing along with my drum. Just a few songs to welcome in the new moon, as tomorrow is the 4th… growth and new beginnings. I have altered my affirmations and she has written hers, ready for the new start. As we say prayers to the directions and open up the energy field, I can feel the energy coming in from the East and Eagle…We play and sing and she begins to see again. I stay quiet, for this time I want her to lead with her heart and she confirms what I see.

At the end of a few songs, as I am directed, I ask if she minds if we sing Kumbaya and then we go off again. It is beautiful to the sound of the drum and rattle, for I have seen her changing and been shown the illusion, as we finish she cries so heartfelt and says I saw Jesus. I know she did, for so did I... but I know you well sweet Lord and it is not I who needs to believe, but others... as emotion sweeps she KNOWS... for the feeling is too strong, for once felt it can never leave. It can never be taken, for the joy that is so immense, it cannot be told... only experienced. We close down with prayers and say thank you to all who joined us here, from Ancestral spirits from the earth and the heavens.

The energy is building fast now, ready for the new beginning at the Garden Station, like Heaven on Earth manifest, as we plant the good seeds. May God Bless you and all that comes through this place for I know... something will be healed within you. You will feel something, for this place is magical...

Good night and God Bless and may the God-ness of the day stay with you. As the universe is a friend.

Always. X

DAY 23

The 4th of April...New Moon and New Beginnings...

Good Morning and God Bless for may the God-Ness of the day stay with you. For the universe is a friend always.

Day 23 and 2 + 3 = 5 and 5 is the number for change, the card of which I pulled last night. Dreams last night again of many - this time going back to my childhood home in Sussex Rd, Coventry. As walking a path I know so well but then I decide to change and go back, not to the safe and the familiar for that I already have experienced but to the truth and the unknown... in trust and faith. I awake with the waves of Ecstasy again, as I throw my arms above my head as they rise and fall like the thunderous storm within. The day comes into awareness... Thursday and a friend, for in God's Love he truly lives and will until the end.

The other friend now fleets in for his energy is felt and known, I can feel him up and about and moving around. It is strange for I can feel him within me and me too within him and I know this... for this is ditto... for we have said before at times... but now it is indeed known. Wondering what the day will bring, I stop myself... I interrupt, nor do I need to know. No, let's enjoy the moment and go with the flow. As I pray and eat as the body talks, the flow begins to build and as I watch the air outside in the bitter cold, the clouds hang again with snow. Here it comes, as it floats down and falls upon the ground then rain alongside to wash the earth, to keep it clean and quench its thirst.

Spices, I place into my cup as I watch it float on the tea... for it is good for me... nourish and rest they say again, time out. For my energy needs to build for a busy time is ahead I feel, somewhere I am going to, the place is not yet known, so I relax in trust and love for God is mine forever home. I pull another card and it says 'safe travel'… I have pulled this for the last week now, most days so it must be so. I shall travel and see many places before I pass over of that I'm sure, so for now, I will place myself in the hands of the Lord and know that I am loved and cared for… as the bigger plan will be show none step at a time.

I must take action though he said, the Swami…as I will get a call from where? He did not say but he did say I must go. That has worried me a little I have to say, not for the unexpected… but if abroad…for I need my health to stay well and my prescription is all I have here. Plus mosquito's like me… very very much!!!

What if I cannot source this? And stay well, will I die? That I must surrender too, for the plan is not of mine. As St Claire of Assisi said in her days of surrender… 'What is to become of me, Lord'…for only he knew? What was her path and which way it would go, right or left, left or right, the crossroads of life? My head spins and I cannot think… is it fear or surrender… as all my earthly pleasures may end forever.

Yet Heaven on Earth is supposed to be the promised land. Manifest… here on Earth… that has been my prayer to the Lord and I am sure it was heard. I believe that God wishes to experience all of everything… through us in his goodness, so surely then I can? I have not yet experienced it all… the proper way. The truth of God's unconditional love, I have seen glimpses… yet still the fullness of this plan is not yet manifested. I do have faith, I do have unconditional love in my heart and I do trust… I go for a walk in the woods as the more I study, the more I appear to realise and the deeper the meaning becomes... not parallel apparently but united as one with God. The seeing becomes more and I need to rest, for this is too much at its very best... the waves increase and it hurts my back and my very being, for my soul cries out... it is like I am suffering.

Hopefully, all will eventually see and realise too, for there is nothing now but to surrender, for there is nothing... The way ahead will be shown, I know it will, for God is good and miracle do occur... Mother Mary said so in a vision. I have remembered that and that I do believe, over anything that man can ever do or say, for they are not leading the way. My heart is open wide as a vessel for all that comes in peace and to 'know' something... I shall always remain this way now, as it has been seen and heard and will not leave me ever.

A friend comes into mind who said to me of late, I had not met with her for many years... but as we sat and chatted as if never apart, she said I can see you now Tracy for I can feel your heart. In Christ, she does believe and in me too, for she said... this is it now for you, for you will never change... not now, and I am proud of you.

Thank you... for your words were heard and gratefully received, for you and so few others on earth truly believed in me, no judgement ever... but love and the seeing of the light. One day you will return to your beloved... and I shall pray for you, for you have truly lived in truth.

***

Tonight I am struggling... struggling to think and yearning for some company which is weird because I struggle when I am in it... so what is the answer apart from balance? Are these days of silence taking its toll? Yet when I wake up to the sound of the birds I love it here, if I could stay in the wilderness with visits occasionally, I would probably be ok.

God is not separate, so I am not alone tonight, yet somehow I feel it… for it is as if no one surely can possibly understand the reality of what I am feeling or are these feelings just mine? I could be feeling someone else in consciousness. To be different is okay and I know that… but tonight it does not feel so… I catch a glimpse of myself walking by in the mirror and although I recognise myself, my reflection is barely recognisable to others…

My ex-husband even walked past me the other day, for he did not recognise me, as the inner is now so changed and reflected in the outer… so tonight I am not sure of how or when I can return to this world but I just have to trust in faith, do not be silly Tracy… This too, shall pass.

The new moon will be out soon so I will have to sing and pray for the greater good of the universe to manifest as quickly as they can… for where, from here I have no plan, no plan at all… I look up the meaning of Kumbaya and apparently, it means to come by here Lord… come by here.

The waves have been on and off all day today, so I think I will meditate again and see if I can contemplate and feel… time out comes back to mind… surrender and just enjoy the moment… so I let go.

Good Night and God Bless for may the God-ness of the day stay with you. The universe is a friend.
Always. X

DAY 24

Good Morning and God Bless for may the God-ness of the day be with you.

I awoke with the Dawn Chorus and immediately remember my dreams, one in particular about the 'Roses' in bloom and the beauty of them everywhere in my garden. A memory flashes up of being surrounded by Roses as a child and how much I loved to look at them, smell them and sometimes try and make perfume out of them from the garage. I adored them, to me they were the most beautiful... The other blossom that I loved as well as our Cherry Blossom tree as it fell on the ground, such a wonderful sight the pink carpet... one of the colours of love and its greatness, its sweetness, its inner beauty and the love I felt for my parents and grandparents as I was truly loved. Today something has changed, for during the night I was being pushed and pulled so hard, as the waves increased so intense in their thunder, as they raged through the physical, my back almost broken under its crash.

At one point I was roused to feel the energy at my head and fought it with all my might... thrashing and hitting out with my hands, for it was the mind... let go my soul cries to release it but it was strong and urging me, as it kept taunting me with fear. But I relaxed and went back to rest, as a mouse squeaked and I clapped my hands to let him know I was near... a sudden thought appeared. Fear is only in mind so let it go... allow the flow and be... your beauty within.

The colours, the flowers, the sounds this morning, all so glorious more than before, the sun shines through the cracks as beams of light, the mist is still upon the woody floor... this sight... this sight I adore. I walk around and connect to every living thing as I cup each flower and plant and tree, I merge with it all, as it lives within me, as we are all birthed from the same creator. Even as I look at the floor, the stones, the iron all of it, for we are all vibrating. The birds, the rabbits, the sky, the clouds as I lift my head and say Thank You... Thank You God, for such another wonderful day. And as I walk back, I look and look again, for things have truly changed. I do not remember that? Or that? Were those bushes hiding it away, like an enchanted garden, a secret one I say.

St Francis and St Clare come to mind...as the story of their life and union as the 'One' soul twin in God's love unfolded yesterday. As I read, I was heartbroken, for I could feel her pain when he had to return, for she was left behind for many years. Like Romeo and Juliet torn apart and yet not, for in their hearts and soul, they rested together in the love and the Lord always. But as told, Clare suffered... for she loved him to the brim, not as other women did but with her very heart and soul for they were in the union and she would have died for him. She would have taken any hit... on his behalf, a bullet through the brain, she would have done, as no one other could.

That love so deep and real, that strength so bold in her commitment to a man... I resonate and think of her bravery for she was the image of him and I bow down to her, in her strength and cry... from the very depths. Oh, God... I remember now, that day we walked together through the crowds to an appointment... As I felt an energy and turned to look behind, a sight appeared so beautiful... a light, there stood a blessed man in his orange gown. I felt his energy as he too felt ours, approaching from his shop.

As we walked by and he came out to see, for he stood... and stared... For with his heart, he could feel ours and the power of two. He smiled at me and I smiled back, for he blessed us then, as much as we are still blessed, now.

But you did not see... for you were distracted by the world. As I continue to walk the woods and sing... my voice has changed as it appears to reach notes not heard before. As a thought springs forth... The love of Christ is so beating in my heart. If I can be saved and move through illusion, then anyone can... After a lovely walk, I reach the shed and suddenly notice the yellow tulips and it moves me... moves me back to tears, for they were dead. My friend had bought them as a gift and I had forgotten to refill their water and they met with certain death. So limp and fragile in their beauty still but I was full of remorse.

For these flowers had already been plucked from their land to die, yet here was I neglecting them in their final days. So I fill their vase with water again and cupped them in my hands. I sent them Reiki healing with my love and asked that they may live again. But nothing... The following day I nearly threw them away... But I tried again and asked with Reiki for their life to return, for it did not look like a drop of water had been drunk... please drink I say, drink from the water of life and live. But nothing... The following day a sign appears as some have started to rise, they are weak but as I cup them again in my hands, as I hold them in my heart and say again.

Please drink and live... for you are truly beautiful and in you, I live too.

Please I beg, as they appear to get stronger, then they start to stand tall in the vase. My heart is glad but also sad for one has not... this one is weaker than the rest. So again I say my thanks to God and to the others... for they are growing again in their beauty, so vibrant in their colour. I cup the weak one, I hold it in my hands... I kiss it gently on its lips of golden yellow. I love you I say, please live again...for you are truly special and as I hear... PRAY... I pray with all my might, for this little one to rise again. This morning on my return, they catch my eye and I smile with absolute delight and then I am moved to tears... For there they all are standing united... tall... together as one, as bright and as beautiful as the day they were given... all of them!

Thank you. Thank You. Thank You. For I am so grateful.

MY DREAMS...

A dream the other night puzzled me for a while as it was about a child... a child with a vest on, who was walking around, going about her life with miniature roses growing under her vest. They were all the colours of the rainbow, as I could see them all. So beautiful yet small, the reds, the yellows, the oranges, the greens, the pinks, the blues, the violets, and the whites all present and growing in their beauty.

Symbolic I thought?

Last night however, they were large everywhere. Roses fully are grown all over a trellis... and bushes of them all planted all around the streets of life mainly yellow ones, as they could be seen, as such a glorious a sight. I said to a woman walking with me how beautiful they were... yet she could not yet see them fully. Oh yes, she said in her indifference, as she knew of a Rosebud not of its significance. I walked beside, half listening to her chat... as I gazed at the secret garden all around me. And listened to what it had to say, so so beautiful in every way...for she was missing out. How blessed was I was the thought that drifted in, for I have been gifted with vision and can see from the heart… Thank You for I would not change a thing, not now.

Another walk this time with Willow the dog in tow… how lovely to have a friend, still silent for she cannot speak… not with her voice anyway but certainly with her eyes as they shine as they look into mine and her tail as it wags so happily on seeing me. I have grown to love her so quickly and I will miss her so much, for she is such a lovely soul. We are joined already… not separate, for in the heart our walks together are heavenly. We venture further into the depths today, through the gate, over the style and on our way, the hills are widespread in their beauty, the land so vast, and a village in the distance… just so precious a sight. For England is the country of my birth and holds such treasure… if we open our eyes to the scenes that unfold around us. People are busy in the village for they cannot see me here but I can imagine them… going about their day scurrying and hurrying, probably worrying their lives away, I can almost hear their thoughts in the consciousness. What do I need for tea? How shall I complete this? Look at that, what a mess? Oh no, this is awful? What do I do now? So many thoughts they have… all in the illusion, for they waste their time on thoughts… that no longer serve them. Not one person was met along the way today and the SILENCE… speaks volumes… for nothing is greater than this.

My soul is leaping like the salmon as we reach a waterfall, a small but deafening one, as it cascades down the hill… moving fast across the rocks and hitting the ground. Such is the sound of water that I love, the movement of one of the most precious gifts of life, for without water and air we would not survive.

A fleeting thought flashes through… priorities… what is important for you Tracy? For some of the best things in life are here and life is meant to be lived to its fullest degree, you know this for having lost a child, you know what love is?

Health…

Family…

Friends…

Animals…

Love of all…

Wealth… for I am the richest woman on earth…

Freedom. True freedom of the sweetest kind.

A wonderful tea was had tonight as I chatted with a couple who turned up by the shed, wanting to speak of their daughter's wedding at the Garden Station in 20:20. A year away but such excitement, for dogs are allowed too… they are so pleased for they are part of their family. They look around and feel the energy, the magic of this wonderful place, as the owner then arrives and confirms it all with them.

They leave so happy, contented in their dreams for their daughters special day and it will be for here, the people are genuine, heartfelt and know of real love… so she will have a very, a very special…and blessed day. Dusk is beginning to fall and I think over last night as I went to bed, I had forgotten… A card I pulled and it said, wish upon a star… so I went outside and looked up but the sky was not clear and there did not appear to be any.

I searched the sky and looked again and there it was just 'ONE', the brightest of them all as it twinkled so bright a light as if to say I Am here. So I said thank you in gratitude and told them all about my dreams, my wishes and then let go for the Angels will carry my words through the universe and they will be known, in the heart of God's love, for the possibilities are endless always.

My energy is high as a new excitement is building within… a change… another shift… I am not sure but whatever it is, it is good… for I can feel it and my soul is alive in the knowing. Day 25 tomorrow. I cannot believe how fast it is going… my life now will include regular periods of silence, as I can see just how much this is meant to be not just time out but connection… direct communication with the Lord is needed every day, for guidance from the greatest teacher and the beloved, so now I know the way, for I can never get lost, not now for it is impossible. Thank You so much, for I am so grateful.

The last walk before bed and the idea of a nighttimes' walk drifts in…I shall arrange it, because then I will really see the animals, the deer, the badger, the fox, the rabbits, the owl and more… when I think to myself?…soon is the reply as I look to the universe and pray.

Good Night and God Bless and may the God-ness of the day stay with you. The universe is a friend.

Always X

DAY 25

Good Morning and God Bless. May the God-Ness of the day be with you.

Well, day 25, for some reason feels like a very good day! As though something is in the air... carried through from yesterday. I am not sure what, for I have had the most disturbing night ever last night. I tried to sleep at 8pm, ok it may be early but when you get up at Dawn Chorus, believe me you are ready. I tossed and turned hour after hour with the waves running through me, not so strong, sweeter but still there constant. At midnight I give up and go outside as the body speaks...and meet with an Owl in fright.

Surely I don't look that bad I say as he wakes up the neighbourhood, with a warning cry... as he tells all. I settle back again and still I cannot drift...a little comes and goes but it feels like someone is thinking of me. Yesterday, April 5th is no special day that I know of. Eventually, I go off but still, I have woken up over and over again, well you need to sleep I say, for goodness sake calm your mind and stop! I awake this morning still to the waves... the 6th nothing I can think of is happening today, for we have cancelled the workday due to an event here at the Garden Station. Probably good for me as I need to rest... my stomach aches and I feel nauseous just like when I used to think I could be pregnant.

Lol... well that would be a miracle... for sure and no one would believe me... no one! My mind drifts to Mary and the immaculate conception... poor Mary, I think that would have been a shame in those days. Just as I had my first born out of wedlock and that was then in modern times, but you would have thought I had committed murder... Pot kettle black for goodness me, I later discover that I was born out of wedlock too, as I surveyed records after my parent's death. Secrets... honestly taken to the grave not only that but much more, just be honest... and live the truth. I suppose they had their reasons as they only wanted better for me.

Gosh, I hope we are not following a pattern... the cycle of repeat, for I have two girls. Lol... watch what you do... and think. I would not care anyway, for what greater gift can God bestow but a child so sweet and pure. One of the greatest gifts of all. For when you look into that new babies eyes and say I Love You, for they are so very very precious. The only word of warning I suppose is that a child is not just for Xmas, as they are for life, just like your animals. The day is still cloudy but the sun will shine through as it usually does... and today I can go out into the world, so I shall.

Something is hanging around my energy field today, now as I walk about in the world, as it has been on and off for the past few days. I have placed a bubble of Angelic love around me and I am not sure why it is getting through, as it is giving me a feeling of heaviness... and flu-like symptoms again. The day passes in a blur and I enjoy my, but this feeling like a cloud will not leave it... I do not think it is me as I have nothing to worry about and my heart was joyful this morning, so it must be in the consciousness. As I take the little one to the park and we feed a robin, she delights at it keeps coming round her pushchair for its food. So beautiful they both are... as they eye each other up! The slide and the swings, the see-saw and me on one end as she laughs hysterically, as I pretend her tiny body is lifting me up into the air... So much joy in the simple pleasures of life.

She knows her own will now, as I try to get her to go down the smaller slide, I can see it in the face. Lol... I will not! She thinks I'm a big girl...

As my heart is in my mouth, as she flies down at speed...

The bus on the way back is full and I still have this feeling of a heart full of lead, not sure why but I need my bed... The world always infringes so I will go into nature and de-stress as my energy needs a boost of goodness.

Good night and God Bless, for may the God-Ness of the stay with you.

Always X

DAY 26

Good Morning may the God-Ness of the day be with you. The universe is a friend.

Today, I think I have definitely caught something or my body is reacting to someone else in the consciousness, for I feel unwell. The bed beckons and regular doses of paracetamol, so I do not think the entry today will be much. I cannot stop crying either…moving through some sort of processing of letting go… as I deserve the best and this was not so.

I make mistakes we all do but at least I will admit it and say so, it is hard when people do not communicate for it is not fair on others not to be honest or at least explain what they feel happened. My love is one of the kindest and most fruitful of all I know this… so if they do not recognise it then it is their issue, not mine. I understand, for maybe they have never experienced it… the truth of unconditional love.

The thought of that man drifts in as his wife is not long passed, I'm hoping he is okay for he has not passed through since. His confidence was good as he just came in and sat down, he knew who he was. Refreshing to see that in anyone and rare… well rounded. Not surprising though as he has done silence too… he obviously 'knows himself well'. This time within the shed will be the making of me. I'm sure, for I will not need to rely on anyone other than myself, as the more days go on, the more I learn about my strengths and weaknesses.

Happy endings, mills and boon and tales of joy have always been my thing and why no… better than any war! I hate to see people a part of you… in the one Consciousness; so what we wish for ourselves, we should want for everyone and everything always. Communication appears to be an issue as people are scared to speak… to be honest… to communicate, so much can be cleared up so quickly and maybe even new and better solutions found.

Perhaps they feel they will be judged but they cannot for if we decide, we too will be judged by God, so nothing to do but communicate in love and care for another human being. As you are always welcome at my house, if you come in peace. Families feuding, so much time lost…she did this, he did that, this was said, I can never forgive them, what a waste…what a waste of precious time and love, for there is never anything that cannot be rectified in open, honest, loving communication… I know this, no matter what your perception.

Married for 30 years and divorced twice to the same man, as we went through much heartache and many changes… I have learnt a lot… especially how to stand in unconditional love. For no matter what, we are still friends and however, he behaves or his perception of things. I just state my version, my truth and we resolve it either to agree or disagree, it doesn't matter for he is him and I am me. Perhaps it is rare because I have learnt along the way to care with an open heart.

Individual personality can get in the way for sure, upbringing and all the more and he can be an idiot… and so have I been many times but if he repeats, I tell him and walk away, for I can't be bothered engage in drama. Deep down, I know he hasn't left because of me as he will not see me homeless… and although I am okay, he will not leave until he knows for sure.

I'm sure that is why, for he will never see me wrong not now, for he has finally learnt something... We made a promise many years ago. Death do us part... and although it is no longer the same, as husband and wife, we know the truth of love... for we both lost our son, a true teacher...of unconditional love. There will not be a third, though we say and laugh, for no more marriage, not to each other anyway. Good God, he says as he shakes his head, you get less for murder!

What about past lives, I say? For I know of three already that we have lived together. Well, when I get back, he says I am to have a word! Because I am not coming back with you, ever again. And he smiles... for I know he would... For this has been a soul contract that he has fulfilled and now he is free... free to go his own way. God Bless, I say for he is loved by God as he has learnt something very important.

After I divorced, I was angry... and my parents came through a medium... he is loved they said, by us all. Blooming cheek... I thought I am your daughter! Lol... but as the medium said more, I knew... I knew in my heart they were right, for we are all the sons and daughters of the Lord. Well, I need to rest for the body speaks and it is weak. All day, drifting on and off... I cannot hold my energy enough, time out the cards say... Okay and no customers pass through, thank goodness for I could not help anyone today but myself.

Good Night and God Bless. May the God-Ness of the day stay with you. The universe is a friend.

Always. X

DAY 27

Good Morning and may the God-Ness of the day be with you.

From the minute of waking, I have been filled with torment today, dreams, tears, longing, hate, it all emerges and there appears to be no end. These last three days, I have cried, felt abandoned, lost, alone and wondering what will become of me in-between such moments of bliss. Is this the balance? I know I am not separated from the one… it is so odd a feeling, of so much love. It is like the mind has gone into absolute chaos, yet in-between it all, the vibrations, the love remains and I know I cannot leave… for this last two years, I have been taken prisoner of some sort of deep joy that will not fade. It will never leave, of that I am sure and even the goodness reduces me to tears, as I look back on my journey, how is this possible?

A child from Coventry, who became a mother and a wife, ends up losing everything, even her own mind? Only to become what… God knows what is to become of me. Thoughts of going to London enter and Scotland to disappear into the streets or the mountains what is it…for sure it is already here within… as I can almost see it… and touch it like a flame that burns brightly, yet invisible to others. Silence they say can send you insane but as I read the books and study more, I see myself within them all, in the truth.

This road… it pulls me like a thirst that cannot be quenched, it is a desert without a well and a field without corn. It is all there is and more and I want to scream and rush back to what I know but I know I can't such is the despair, for only God can guide me to wherever I will end up. I feel like I am being stretched on a rack… from the earth to the heavens… the root beckons but so does the crown, for it wants to reach up higher and higher.

Assisi enters my mind and the pilgrimage that must take place. I need to pray for the only way to get there will be through Gods Grace, not mine. The feeling of wanting to contact my friend fleets in, the magnet, for I am sure there is something that he knows that he has kept hidden from me... I want to shout at him too and beat my fists upon his chest for if he knew... why did he not warn me.

Or was it that I prayed to God that time. That he would be saved and I would suffer for him... Such is the feeling of death in the living... I have to breathe for I have been becoming weaker these past three days, sick in body as the chest is heaving and a heavy cough prevails, a headache and slow... energy. Yet... I feel well so how contrary is that? As I walked through the woods and felt the breeze, I could have laid down and died there and then, I would not have cared, for I know that this is real.

Swami comes to mind...I shall link in and see if he hears me for he has visited before, maybe he will return, for I am sure I need some guidance, yet God is the guide not the man! God is already here... in the moment, all the time in my heart... it is so weird, for before I used to pray and think he would need to hear me but now I know it just needs to be felt, the feeling in my heart for that is true communion. Three times I have slept today...as rest is required, a little food, olives, cheese and cashews, grapes, banana and a slice of seeded bread. Lemon and honey in hot water and the feeling of the physical being nourished is good.

Listen to the body... but if I do... I need human touch today, a cuddle... but there is not one to be had, so I hold myself in my arms with love. My cards, they speak of victory... The victory of what? For every day, the card comes out. Once before this happened many years ago, when I was waiting for the result of something that was breaking me... and it did occur, the miracle!

Whatever it is, I hope it is soon... I have had dizziness on and off for the past few days, it appears unrelated to my cough, as it is a feeling of energy not physical. Space appears to have opened up in my head...a sense of emptiness... is it the mind disappearing or the crown opening? But it is a new feeling, a sensation like no other experienced before. Another sleep, I am drifting in and out of consciousness, I'm sure... no dreams, just rest and my body feels so cared for.

The empty feeling is still present in my head, it feels good, much better than before...lighter. We appear to move through shadow into the light, for one dream rears its head from the other night and I want to kill... how can I have this feeling of hate again but I do, so I forgive myself and them again and again as it no longer serves me. What a terrible thing to know hate... no wonder there is war. I am blessed however with common sense and know that love is all there is as they are the same as me inside, with different dreams but we are still the same, born of the same and will return to the same, so I let go let go of it all.

The waves have flowed all day today... gentle... the deep hum of the OM, resting in the arms of the beloved. I saw my parents earlier and then my son and nephew. My Nan and pap and aunt and uncle, plus two more... As if they have called by as if to say 'we are here'... you forget to speak with us and ask us for assistance, as we bring the Angels too and I can see one. So I ask for help and drift off... back into sleep. The lighter nights are upon us now, as each one extends... it is now 8:20 and I can still see... the owl has started hooting so it must be nearly time for bed. Last night I was woken up quite late with the roar of a motorbike in the pitch black, as it came thundering through the wood with screams of lads.

I quickly switched off the tiny lamp and lay still, no fear entered because I thought if you were to come into my little home, you would get a bigger shock on seeing me. For up above I have an iron hook, on a very heavy piece of wood. Three little pigs jumped to mind in the wooden house but this time the power animal, the wolf is inside.

Can you imagine their faces if they saw me… and wielding this? I think they would run long before I did, so fear does not overtake… and they zoom off after standing chatting only an inch from me, if only they knew.

Well, I am starting to feel brighter, the body has turned a corner and hot bread and butter pudding is eaten with cream, delicious. I am living the noble life of a pauper… and happy to do so, for this has been one of the best experiences of my life! As I know, I can make a home anywhere… As I walked earlier, I saw a large hole under a bridge, an old flume from many years ago. It looked like a cave, a little hobbit house or a home for me if needs be, as I am happy anywhere that God decides I need to be and I will always follow the direction.

A conversation comes back into play with my shamanic teachers over the weekend, their love and encouragement, as I ask a question about an occurrence, as I was not sure if I was supposed to feel this happen. They are honouring you Tracy, they said… the ancestors, for what you are doing is very rare and not many will ever venture that far. Thank You, I said for I am proud of myself and how I am

177

managing even when at times it feels dark. Keep going they mean, for you are nearly there and you will reach your destination.

We are with you... every day in thought and love they say... I am so blessed to have these people in my life, thank you God, for sending them my way. A drawing falls upon the floor, a gift from another friend who woke up in the night before my return up north and had to quickly put the vision to paper, so beautiful it is, three elephants in a row, one red, one orange and one yellow, all walking together.

She drew her vision for me, to stay in strength... to keep me focused she said and secure on my path... for you may be tested but you have such inner strength and you can do it! For where you are going, only God knows but it is special... Thank you for believing in me too, for the steps do appear one by one as you said and all I have to do is follow them.

Sleep is calling me now, so I bid you goodnight. Sleep well and have good dreams...

Goodnight and God Bless and may the God-Ness of the day stay with you. The universe is a friend.

Always X

DAY 28

Good Morning and may the God-Ness of the day be with you. The universe is a friend.

The body is still weak and the cough prominent but the vibrations are thunderous...I can see Green and Violet and White light so bright, like Angels as I say out loud and pray... God help me! At this moment... as I sob and sob, trying to make sense of it all... but I cannot, for there is nothing but surrender for me. Death... it must be... For I remember seeing my sons face as he sat up and looked towards the heavens... in his dying breath. His face was so beautiful as a light of an 'Angel' as he smiled and let go of our hands for he needed us no more. He was an enlightened one.

I saw... for he outstretched his arms towards another father... so happy was the joy, as it shone from him, I saw the love, I saw the light. So bright in his heart, as he was raised again. What is to become of me, I say... I am truly pathetic, an ant has more strength than me a mere human... useless.

These feelings as they all run through... I can feel every desire rushing through me so violently as to send me insane... everything over and over as if all 'wants' for eternity are to be met, right now in this very second.

The body jerks and again space emerges...something is pushing through so strong that it will not stop, for it is outside of everything but God... It must be, as it is so powerful. The universe turns within...a shift, like the cosmos turning and whirling... a change... which brings with it a sudden feeling of freedom like never before.

It feels as if I swim naked in the sea and allow the curl of the waves to unfold around me... just lying... on the current, in nothingness... allowing it to take me to wherever. The sun breaks through into the shed and I see the world, hear the birds and know 'Love' for this is real, so real it is untrue, yet not, for I know it in my heart as the heart speaks and thuds. For the lick of Love is both slick and still. Tender and sweet as it consumes... until it has had its fill... for I am helpless in its arms, in its breath in its everything as I merge with 'The One'.

A normal life I say to myself what is one of those? For mine has disappeared into another dimension. It is like I am waiting for a roundabout as a child to jump on... But this must be a magic one, to take me around in a circle to a new place, a new life, a new home, a new everything, for there is nothing here of any recognition nothing... Yet I am not scared at all, for everything is as it is meant to be, as I have faith so strong and it will care for me always. I have to enter the world for an hour or two today as a funeral is being held and I have said I will sit with the owners grand children.

Only two hours out in the world and it has disturbed me already, for now I doubt, as I hear my friends words come to taunt me... Do you think you need therapy? I could smack him hard. For never once did I ever doubt him...not once, yet here I now doubt myself because of another. It hurts so much for did he not care a bit for me, so much for the friendship, he did not know the meaning of. He would not have laid himself bare to protect me like I did him... or sacrificed himself for me. God knows what is in my heart always and in that I trust. I sob and sob again for I have to let go of this, I am worth so much more... so much.

Mr. Celebrity... I was harsh maybe! But maybe you needed it to be... what happened to you... was it the suites or did I support you too much and make you think that you were so amazing that ego reigned above all common sense? For I know of your intelligence and it is great, so where... where is the common sense. For humility... was once an attribute that I so loved in you... and the man.

Years ago, when I went to London and was starting to look at learning as part of the Brahma Kumari's you were there... where? For we both surely forgot their teachings. To be kind always, compassionate, not harsh... but maybe a taste of your own hard medicine. For if you complain... you will be complained about... for it is how we behave towards each other as part of the human race, remember we are all the same... soul signatures. Reap what we sow... we all need to remember this.

We cannot judge, for no matter how hard we have chosen to work, that is our choice, not theirs and we do not know what goes on in the lives of others. Even if we do pay well for a service...who knows how they are feeling today and what occurs in suffering, so if you have to say a word, let it be a good one, to encourage, not chastise or belittle as they turn away, for they can still hear you, for they are not deaf and it hurts their heart. It doesn't matter what you think. Don't do it...turn around, before it's too late, for I hate to see you hurt yourself, be compassionate for yourself and others, for when one day you will look down at your own feet... you will hear and see again what you said... for I know you and you are good... you are... for I can see it... truly I can.

As the poem goes... The child who grows up with criticism... learns to condemn. Spirit showed me once that the road to money is filled with potholes…and it will fall under your weight unless you get the balance straight; for you cannot be a noble prince until you can be a noble pauper. I am far from an idiot and far from dim… I know how to listen and to listen only to him in 'Love'. Love is greater than any man and will lead me to pastures green. As I go for a walk…

The deer at the top of the hill stands proud, he is made from iron and surveys the land, I love him so… I stand and merge with him holding onto his back as though I could ride him… for he is truly noble, majestic the King of the animal kingdom. This evening is calm and beautiful as I sit for a while and enter the space of oneness with nature. The bridge catches my eye and the way over to the hobbits house, so I go, step by step staying in the middle, as I don't like heights and there are no sides. As I reach the hobbits house, I can now see it from here in all its glory, it is perfect I think and I could manage.

My plan begins, to remove the rubble and use wood to block up both ends, then I realise there is a hole in the roof, all the better to see the stars with I think to myself. But what about the rain, a piece of Perspex maybe would suffice… what a wonderful home it would make, only enough room to sleep but it would be just fine. I smile to myself and think I would be happy if the weather stayed warm, for I could live out here always… in the most beautiful home of all God's kingdom. As I go to retire, the feeling of warmth comes over me and flashes of my life pass through from a small child, memories aplenty like being shown a cine camera reel.

I was one of the more fortunate ones… I try to sleep but still the memories are shown over and over… aged 3 being taken to the park to go on the rowing boats with nanny and pappy in their black vintage car with red leather seats. I can see myself sitting in the back and my pap talking to me. The harmonica and the little glasses that we used to play shops with. More and more flash by, so much so that I wonder if I have a life review. Maybe something will occur tomorrow?

Who knows but I accept whatever my destiny is. The Owl is hooting and I am tired as this cough is still persistent, the headache returns, so I gratefully lay in my bed happy in my little shed, my home.

Good Night and God Bless and may the God-Ness of the day stay with you. The universe is a friend.

Always. X

DAY 29

Good Morning may and the God-Ness of the day stay with you. The universe is a friend. Always.

I awake at Dawn Chorus with a hacking cough and start to pray to heal myself of this, I use Reiki and the Grace Symbol for maybe there is something that is holding on to me… a past covenant perhaps. As I say that I see in my mind's eye a chain and an iron clamp around my ankle, maybe I was a slave… so I send the symbol down my lineage and ask for release.

All night I have had flashes of memories coming through, so I am sure this has been a life review. I am hot maybe I have a temperature, so I think about sitting up in bed but I cannot, for the top of the bed is open. My dad suddenly appears in my mind as I look around the shed and immediately I am shown the solution, I get up and place my therapy bed against the head of the bed, so I now have a padded headboard. He was a genius, I am sure my dad as he could build, design, draw, he could do and solve anything but common sense… not a lot he had, such a shame.

It feels sublime as I make tea and sit up in bed with my pillow behind me wondering why I didn't see it before, I open the curtains and watch the sun come up as the birds sing and flit about… How lucky am I. It is then I hear it, a song that spirit sing so loud that you would think I have a radio. They sing it so proud…

God save our gracious Queen, what I think? I don't even know the words but it bellows out… The word 'Passed'… shoots to mind, I wonder if they are telling me I have passed something? Of what though I am not sure, apart to know that if I had to remain here forever… I would not care for I am happy. The observatory, the stars I suddenly think of, as last night was such a bright and beautiful night, they twinkled like diamonds… To reward myself, I believe after my 40 nights, I will go into the village and stay in a BnB, in a bed… so soft and luxurious… for two nights, as I am technically still homeless.

Then I can go to the observatory at night and see the stars under the dark sky of Northumberland. My son needs me on Wednesday to stay over whilst he goes to London filming, so that is another night and there is always the shed until I get to the barn for two weeks. Well, that's the plan my plan for now, but who knows what may occur.

Now tea and hot buttered toast beckon as I am delighted… that I can sit up in bed, all snugly and enjoy it…what a treat! Well, today has been a real day of contrast as I have felt so ill, I could barely leave my bed and succumbed to lay in until I thought I had better move, for anyone finding me will think I'm dead. My body has felt like lead… unable to move, my legs and my back aching so much. The tablets appear to have given up, like me. I slowly emerge and have lunch… vegetable soup and cheese on toast which I relished. Nourish… it helps I said.

There have been many tears today, as this second half appears harder than the first, yet not in some way. I walk the woods in floods and wonder why it all comes up, it must be something to do with the silence, as it clears us on an intense level. My head is hurting so badly that I place a hot pan of water in front of me and sniff the steam, as I am so chesty yet no cold, it is weird. Yet my body shakes as though I am freezing. I am left wondering how the homeless manage, especially in the winter for they would surely die from health-related problems. Jack springs back to mind again, a homeless man I met as he was in trouble, I could see it and he needed help. So I gave him some money and told him to get on a bus for his legs were weak and he needed attention. Because I cared, he cried as I held him in my arms and in my heart as I placed my hand upon his and sent him so much love... I have never forgotten.

Just one day I think today, I would I love to see my father again, to speak with him and say all the things we should have said before he passed. We did a lot and most of it was satisfied, as we had time but I think there was still a little more and I love you dad so much... I say today, for you were good. As I sit outside the shed, as the sun has come out and warms my aching bones, I see a man and do a double take... for it looks like him. The same coat, the hat, the walking stick, he sometimes took on rambles for he was a rambling man. He even walks the same, with the tilt of the head everything, it is weird I said. I forget about him and then later go back out into the woods for no one is around and it is quiet. I turn a corner and go up a hill and there nearby, not too far way he stands... looking at me as I look at him. The features even look the same, I want to speak with him but I think, do not be silly, for you may frighten him, an old man out on a ramble.

He walks some more and stops again and even still the mannerisms... it is weird... as a feeling hits me so hard in the heart and I hear 'I love you too, Tracy'.

Jesus, I must be hallucinating as I've been so ill but I know that spirit can manifest in what appears the physical. For I have seen it before with a young child, for no one could see him but me, or so I thought. And as he crossed the fairground in front of me and walked towards our post of our son's cafe, as he went behind, he did not come out the other side. His mother, I had thought had forgotten him but she must have lost him, like I lost a son, for I knew he was hers. My foster son with learning difficulties saw him too, because he said he was wearing a football shirt and this I knew. In my previous book, I speak of this and many will probably think I am crazy but never doubt, for you never know until you see the truth. As I walk back to the shed, a butterfly appears, bright blue spots on red... so beautiful... so much pleasure in life.

The Phone Call...

I suddenly remember to ring my ex-husband, as he said to ring today. For he would know about a place, he thought. The council have been good, he said but it will take at least three months and they said I would have to go into a hostel. I laughed so loud for 'knowing him'. For he said to the woman, you can bugger off... not being horrible but I will sleep in my car if I have too.

As she exclaims with a shriek, you cannot do that... you will have too! I can just imagine the conversation flowing between the two, I bet he wishes now he'd have taken that transfer. Well anyway, within an hour he has found a place and sorted it out for himself, a 2 bed bungalow, he said with a garage for storage and a little garden. As he goes to say it, I see it in a vision and cry, just as he says, it looks a bit like your dads.

I used to love my dad's bungalow and would often go to stay for I loved the garden and the energy there, as it was always so peaceful. I have nothing he said to put in it but a bed each and I have taken on extra hours so you will be okay to stay, for you cannot be homeless. Thank you again. I say for it is good that we have remained as friends... Oh, do not worry; he says loudly, I am never coming back with you ever again... You are way too much trouble!

I am so grateful though, as I know you did not have to and I appreciate it very much, so thank you but like the time you were taken to hospital, I was the first one at your side, like divorce or not I would not see you wrong and when I had my car crash... you drove all the way up to Scotland to collect my friend and me and although there was someone who would have helped... You did it without so much of a thought, so, Thank You.

I quickly ring my sister and a couple of friends, for he does not even have a tea towel! So if they are throwing anything out that could be useful... and if he has it already, I will donate it to the homeless. This has definitely been a topsy-turvy day, for now he gets the keys on the 26th... I am away, caring for my friend's home and still in silence for a little while, as I am looking after the barn until the 13th May, for I need to reintegrate slowly... bit by bit, back into the world.

Thank you, God for everything today, for I trusted you in complete faith and I knew it would sort itself out! The thought of a bed in a centrally heated place is such a luxury that I cannot believe, my... how much things have changed. My tea was eaten and now I'm exhausted not just with the feeling of 'ill' but I think the relief of it all has taken its toll. Because as much as I trust and I know I could happily live in the hobbits house, it's nice... to have the choice, not to have to. I have thought before about living in a cave at the seaside and living off what the sea washes up... well that's a thought but I had better be careful! Lol... Tiredness beckons as the tablets are starting to work, as a change to another sort has helped, the bones are not so bad except when the cold eats into them.

I shall snuggle down and say Goodnight for I really need to sleep tonight and hope this leaves me. I AM well! I reinforce it to myself and have faith that it believes me. One thing at a time Tracy, one thing at a time…or step as they said.

Day 30 tomorrow… can you believe it? I can't.

Good Night and God Bless and may the God-ness of the day stay with you. The universe is a friend.

Always X

DAY 30

Good Morning and may the God-Ness of the day be with you. The Universe is a friend.

Dawn Chorus and as I awake, all sorts of thoughts are fleeting through and have been all night, especially about the man I saw yesterday, walking in the woods. He had a quality about him, a quality that puzzled me and as I watched him walk as I could see, he was walking so mindfully. The feeling overcame me of Jesus… in his love and this air, this air of supremacy.

It is not a certain kind anymore that you will attract, for those lessons have been learnt, it is the King fit for the 'Queen'. One who knows himself well.

For only periods of inner contemplation can give this to him, as they have to you. The years of hard inner work, clearing out and working through shadow. The One who knows how to behave and when they have stepped over the line, into their inner child or whatever aspect of themselves, they can quickly turn around. And the one who can treat you in the same way as you treat them, with so much unconditional love… I hope he calls by again, I think for I shall go and walk with him. I now do not think this man was old, I think he was dressed for the weather and was in silence, for what I was seeing was an old soul, a wise one, a sage who can see.

Thank you God, for hearing me… I trust in you and have faith that all is well for I have been waiting, waiting so long for this day in God's Love. So I will welcome him into my kingdom with so much love, for it is you and only you that knows whose best… A match made in heaven… another half…the soul signature ready for the return to the God Head. I can see it… and I trust it all… Thank you, for you will not forsake me, for I have worked too hard and I am so very loved.

My neck is stiff this morning and I still have a headache, this cold still has not come out and I do not want it to turn within… as I need to reach the promised land. So thank you, I will pray long and hard today, I AM Healthy of Mind, Body and Soul. I AM Healthy of Mind, Body and Soul. I AM Healthy of Mind, Body and Soul. So be it! The birds come by my window as I eat my breakfast, for in my thoughts, I have forgotten theirs… Oh, I am so sorry I say, as I quickly run to collect the bread, the seeds and the sultanas.

The blue tit cocks her head and looks at me, so beautiful is she… Also the Thrush, he seems annoyed with me and gives me a long hard stare because he cannot find anything in his bowl.

Bless him… I won't be long I say, as I go around the three places and fill them back up. They look so happy with the offerings that I place at their table… no matter how small, they are grateful for everything. As I finish my breakfast, I get a flash of a vision, of me sitting at a table eating, the best crockery, lovely china, a lovely teapot and only the best, only the best will do as fit for a Queen. Gosh, I am linking into someone he will treat me well for he realises my worth. What a lovely man and this will be returned to you, my friend… two-fold.

My neck is starting to release now and I am feeling so much better, a walk today in the sun will do me a world of good. For the sun has come out, the sky is blue and I feel so much lighter, as further space has opened up within my head. Thank God… My body has surrendered to the greater plan.

I feel quite excited as I have the strength now to pull my wellington boots on, get ready and off I go into the wilderness… The feeling of love, the waves have returned yet in a peaceful way, so beautiful it is today, in flow. A little thud of the heart now and again but nothing much and like butterflies in the stomach… The feeling of Love. As I relax and enjoy the feeling… for it is here. What a wonderful walk was had, my heart feels lifted… as I turned the corner to go up the hill and there she stood in all her finery… The Deer… Majestic, soft and gentle, a beautiful soul, she did not move but watched me well. She looked at me as I at her and tears fell, for her beauty is no other than I have ever seen.

A Queen…

We stood for quite a while and then as it was time to go… she turned as I did but I turned back to see her leave and it was a beautiful sight, for the grace of this animal is so divine, such is the delight… and as her white behind bobs in the distance I laugh, for then I think she looks like a giant bobtail rabbit. I walk on further to an unknown land and sit upon a log, the view is taking my breath away and I sigh… such a sigh of love.

I hear a conversation being played… where would you like to go? How about the Highlands, was my reply, or maybe Western. Have you been? Have you seen? My chatter grows as I am now not only excited, I am seeing it and feeling it too. I will be shown places that I have never seen and so will he. It is like a dream but a beautiful one of which will manifest, for I can feel it in my heart… as it rests in the hands of the Lord. But I have nothing I say…nothing at all, to offer you but unconditional love, so if that is enough then take your fill, for you are welcome.

My pockets both have holes in now, a sign I am sure, for it had been said I cannot take anything home no matter what. No change, no notes, no nothing but the 'Love' that lies within my heart, for the rest belongs to the earth.

As I approach the shed again, another song comes forth…We Three Kings of Orient Are… Bearing Gifts… I had heard this for a few days now before they used to sing 'Go West' as it in is my journal and I used to wonder what it meant. It appears to be coming back again, as in three kings it also says westward leading.

A puzzle to which the answer will be shown…in Divine Timing. But, at this present moment I feel so happy for I keep seeing myself in different places, by the sea, up in Scotland, abroad, all over, as there is so much fun to be had in each and every moment, for he will treat me well for he knows… he knows the truth, this man and he knows my worth. Liquid Gold runs through the veins of every man, woman and child but we have to source it like the gold diggers did so many years ago, it is there, it is just hidden from us all to rediscover by going deeper and deeper within. The scriptures across all lands are helping all of them but the real truth is what lies within.

I think tonight, I will sit up high by the Iron deer and watch the sun go down, for I am feeling so much better now. Thank God. 'I AM healthy in Mind, Body and Soul' has been my chant. OMG… A sudden thought shoots in… We Three Kings… Lol… I was only joking the other day with my friend and saying Men are like buses… they have the tendency to turn up all at once! How funny that would be, as it would be like the olden days… of suitors.

Well only 'The One' will get through, for God will see to that, like cupids arrow! I think the universe has a laugh… they are teasing me because I have worked so hard, not just this 40 days and nights but in the past two years and now… now we will be having so much fun!

I have just realised something else… Today day 30 for 3 is an angelic number and a 0 is a circle for the circle of life, the infinity and can also represent, everything comes around again in the hands of time. Also it is the 11th, a double-digit… the infinity and new beginnings, plus the power of two standing side by side.

Plus, I have just added up the date and month and the year and it rounds down to 9 for completion…the absolute… a Divine number, how much more confirmation do you need! God, I think I need a lie-down… Lol, a nap… zzz… for I need to get my rest in, for when he arrives we will be busy… SEEING & GOING PLACES! Honestly, I can read your minds, those of you reading this book, haha for I know what you were thinking as I shake my head… so funny, x.

***

A sudden occurrence.

An experience occurs at around 7pm for I am jumpy. Very jumpy, for I can feel that something has either occurred or is about to. I go outside and look around but all is quiet, I quickly seal the perimeters and place up a bubble of love all around. I feel as though I am going into a state of trance, so I decide to go back in, lie down and meditate. I quickly light a candle as now I can feel and see, a vision of the distress of a friend. I send out all the powerful energy I can and suddenly I see both of my shamanic teachers arrive in my little room. Their guides and mine too, Black Elk, White Buffalo Calf Woman, Brown Bear, all of our ancestors, your family, mine, and the angelic realms. As they suddenly shot in from nowhere to assist you and asked me to lead, so I kneeled at my shrine, my altar to take instruction and within seconds we rush to your aid.

All of us standing united together in our power helping you, for they cannot hurt you, it is not allowed... I see the pain, the years of their darkness, trying to trick you, to infringe upon your soul but they cannot, for now you are empowered in the truth. I quickly turn you around and cut many many cords, snares that they have bound around you... not just in this life but many others. Be gone... I shout firmly for they cannot stay... for they are banished, never to return. Their souls are screaming as they cry out, I see them rise and fall, writhing in their energy, for they are lost... lost in their darkness of pleasure and pain... I cast them out, we all do for you are free to rise again.

Their souls need to be saved, so I have asked for Gods help because they need it so much, for their free will has become their darkness and in their hour of need I will not turn away but you are to be cut free, forever today.

I see it happen as you suddenly rise up high and I set you free too to fly, wherever you need to go. Fly high, I say over the mountains and far away, in all my love and with all my blessings, for you are the Eagle too and you must... Fly.

Just as I finish the ceremony, with my drum and dance, as called to do so. I hear the chants of the choir of the brothers... so sweet a note, so blessed and it enables me to float, to float up high into the golden light. I merge with you and allow the 'Love' to flow... Alleluia they sing...I see you crying and praying, praying with all your might but do not stress I say, for you are saved tonight.

All is well, as you sit in love in my father's kingdom with me, for you are safe and you are forever liberated, for you have done far more good than you have ever done bad. Archangel Michael, Gabriel all of them have been, for we are so blessed and Christ of course... for he will never leave you... never. Do not fear for I am always here and everything is not always as it seems. For sometimes an earthquake has to happen to take away the old and replace it with the new, a better, clearer, clean and stable foundation, based on truth and not on fabrication.

Remember... the right people are always in the right place at the right time and all will be well. I say a heartfelt thank you to all who suddenly came in, as I was not expecting anything. As I was getting ready to retire. As they suddenly shot in from nowhere to assist. So now I kneel again as I say my prayers of gratitude, so much gratitude, for today has been a good day and I shall continue to stand in Love, Grace & Truth with Balance & Peace in my heart. Blessings to you... always.

Goodnight and God Bless for may the God-Ness of the day stay with you. The universe is a friend.

Always X

DAY 31

Good Morning and may the God-Ness of the day be with you. The universe is a friend always.

I awake with the Dawn Chorus and I have had a good night better than a while, as my cough is leaving me now, as I draw back the curtain to sit with my tea. The robin, the chaffinch, the blue tit, the blackbird, the thrush, the raven, the pigeon I see them all as they fly by or stop at my window. Just then I see it coming, it is a Heron… I love them, as it flies directly at the side of me.

Amazing I think as I watch it closely, I quickly turn on my laptop for I cannot remember their spiritual meaning but how funny when I realise for it said, 'The Heron is the representation of stillness and tranquility and once these are in place, opportunities are recognised further. Also a sense of independence. As I think about it now, the Blue Tit has been following me around and also calls by my window every morning, as I look this one up too, I am surprised but not really as everything unfolds. For it says seeing a Blue Tit is about Love and Trust and an omen that Love is on its way. That a partnership will be the very best, for the person who represents this is a true and honest match a lifelong and honourable person.

Noble and faithful who will stay by your side until your dying day, for there will be no other for them. Like the Swan, for once they decide to enter a relationship, they will only have one mate for life. How funny, I think as based on messages I received the other day, how lovely confirmation is… I know this because I can feel it, he is on his way for it is now embedded in my heart the 'feeling'. The King fit for a Queen, for apparently he is stable and will woo me…

Now that I do look forward to, as I am a hopeless romantic, as he will recognise my worth and me his.

New Beginnings…

As I have switched on, a message flashes up from my ex husband…The bungalow has fallen through for she said the council wanted safety certificates… so I reply. Ok do not worry for it was not meant to be, she had put up the rent too, by quite a lot by the time you viewed and was judging you, so let it go. For there is something better on the horizon and it is not where I thought I saw you be. He rings back after a short while and says the council have said he is a priority for another place near to where he works, which is where I saw in my vision, so I am sure this is correct. I will know next week he says and if not I have a few more privately to view, one of which is already empty. Whatever is meant to be will be, as I say do not panic, I will pray and you will get the right place for you.

Every time I have contact with the outside world, something changes, even this writing style on my laptop for I have not touched anything but it is different. Keep up Tracy I think, this is not you that is determining the path, it is the universe as it turns… I have been laughing at myself this morning, looking back at old behaviours from my younger days, as I most definitely was not the same as I am now. I did not have the same patience at all in any way or the same level of trust, although I will say I did always think there was something greater than us. My friend fleets to mind and I laugh hysterically now at the remembrance of the day, as we got up to leave and I turn to him and say,

"Now you don't need the toilet, do you?""No," he says indignantly as 'The mother' aspect in me rears her head… Lol. Well just thank god my granddaughter was not old enough at the time for watching TV. Because, I would have surely said in such a soft & lowly voice, "Do you need the toilet train, Bing."

So funny how we go on automatic pilot, without a thought... that would have ended any friendship... haha...But sure enough, because I know for halfway around the block, he stops and says I need to find a toilet. Oh, God... I am sure a man was invented to try the patience of a Saint... haha or to make one. Later on, he turns to me and says, "You have the patience of a Saint!"

Think yourself lucky, I say for I never used to have... my children were chased around the house in the early days but I could not catch them. My husband too, so funny it must have looked...and no we not playing games, for I was mad and full of hell and if I could have just caught them... The neighbours would have tales to tell, for once I chased my husband with a stick outside into the garden, how embarrassing... I could have surely killed him! And as he ran inside again and slammed the door so hard... the lock dropped. So now I get more and more annoyed, as I see red and the steam must have risen from 0 to a 100 in a second.

For now, I cannot get in... so I start like a mad woman, thrusting the stick through the letterbox, faster and faster, as I shout louder and louder... Open this door right now and let me in!!! Would you have let me in? I know, I blinking wouldn't .Lol! Oh dear, shocking I am... and certainly not a Saint for I have many a tale that I can tell, as I learnt my lessons. So you see I don't really know what God sees in me, for if I am made in the image and likeness of him... he must have used Adams funny bone to make me. Haha... The message 'Know Thyself Well'. Ah the dog has escaped and has come to visit me, how lovely so I let her in... for a morning cuddle, for she is just so beautiful. I switch on the fire and we snuggle down for five minutes before I have to take her home.

She is always so happy to see me, for unconditional love for sure they give... and I love her too so much. The day has passed quickly today, as I went for a walk in the woods and decided to sit beneath a tree. I sat with my back to its trunk as I could see the view across the field and a farm on the other side. A beautiful cob horse, black and white came to take stock of the new view and as the sun came through, I could see the bright rays filtering through my eyelids.

Meditation in nature is beautiful, as I feel the earth and connect, heal yourself now this last part of anything that no longer serves you and releases it down into the earth through the roots... imagine it is turned into compost for the goodness of the earth, as I visualise my energy pushing further and further through the soil. It was so comfortable, as the ground was mossy and as I watched a couple walk down the main part of the wood, as being up high they would not notice me... as silence does that. It makes you want it more funnily enough, not less.

As people suddenly become like invaders in your garden, no matter where you are in the wilderness. I like people, very much but silence does something, as you also love your own company too and are happy.

It is that inner happiness that some speak of... finally it arrives. I had taken a travel cup of hot chocolate and that must have done it. For... that was the best sleep I've had in a while, for I fell right off into a deep sleep! Can you imagine that if anyone would have found me? Do you think they would have woken me? Probably, for I bet I was snoring. I do not remember nodding off but I was still in the same position when I awoke, wish I could have taken a selfie!

People fleet in and out of the woods today and I am still in need of rest, for this illness has taken some energy away. I shall have to replenish more and more until I am full again, drink more juices as well packed full of vitamins for I need a shot of zing.

That message did say time out and as my time is soon to finish… just enjoy it Tracy I think, for everything and everyone will still be there long after you are gone. My head does feel lighter, I have to say as though there is so much space, especially all around the back and top now, maybe that rat did get in and take my mind away with him.

MESSAGE

Just enjoy the moments and enjoy yourself being you, in your authenticity for it is beginning to really shine through. I am so grateful for without the love and support of the Garden Station would I have made it? This time in silence with their support has been worth its weight in Gold for me… better than any lottery. So much better, for money can only buy you freedom of some degree, it cannot bring you inner happiness, no matter how much you think it will. However, once you find that and put it in place, the money is a bonus, as you can do whatever then, travel, assist others, be of service, so many things as your authentic self.

I would love that… to see money being put to so much goodness… as money is not the root of all evil, it is what a human does with it in their free will experience, if they are not ready. Money is made from the earth, especially the note from a tree and what is more beautiful and full of wisdom… we should take note as Trees have stood for thousands of years… and keep us alive. We cut them down, kill them and spend them, we heat our fires, build our houses and more and not once do we ever say 'Thank you' as we continue to take much more than we need.

For we should remember everything and to be so so grateful for it all, no matter how small. This is the time, funnily enough when I feel the money would be a bonus, for I see people 'suffering' as their lives twist and turn at the hands of fate and just think how sometimes it would be lovely to help them, as I was helped in the past. But do I think I learnt all my lessons at the time, probably not for I really didn't look at what was happening… But the day I took responsibility for my own thoughts, my own decisions both good and bad was the day that things started to change for the better.

I know through my own experiences that once out the other side things are transformed but at the time it is sometimes so hard to find blessings in your current situation. To be able to let go of the outcome, for when we do, often the happier ending appears a lot quicker than if we hold onto the drama and buy into it. It is not easy and my goodness I know that myself… but for people who manage to achieve it… their lives shift…as if by magic… When I was under the grip of a nightmare… in my life, every day, I had to hold onto my thoughts and keep them only positive. It took nearly 9 months before the resolution appeared and it was so hard, for fear gripped every cell of my very being.

But minute by minute, I cast it out and did not allow doubt to creep in. I looked at the positive that I had around me and clung to that in the hope, the trust and the faith that all would eventually end well and it did.

Apparently, 9 months is very fast I was told, for it could have hung on in our case, hanging in the balance for years... but I did all that I could and no more, as I knew I had to let go of the control for all the choices had been taken away from me. Every day I prayed and did my cards and prayed some more, only taking action when either something was asked of me or if something was shown until finally, it happened.

I wrote a date down in my diary on April 22nd and that was the day of my miracle. I am not sure if I believe in Karma as being permanent but I think more of lessons to be learnt, to make us stronger and more stable, more balanced as people but I now think we can change this quicker than what we think we can. As like reap what you sow is a similar thing, for the day you do more good or have more good thoughts than the other, is the day that the scales of justice tip in your favour. In the meantime, though you have to stay as still as you can, in all situations and as peaceful in the flow within, allowing any bumps in the road to just blow over.

And like wispy clouds I say, if you see something coming towards you, see if it will float away over your head and if not, do what you need to do but only the minimum. Then go back to staying still within in peace, for your behaviour will determine the outcome. It takes practice... If you cannot change it... leave it and let it go, do not give it too much attention. If you can do anything do it... but the smallest tweak and then wait... see... and if no further movement occurs, take action on the next step that appears.

The problem with what I am saying here is the human condition... for we all get into fight mode, justification or victim, as the emotions rise or anger appears, old behaviours resurface, we can hide away from it, drink ourselves into oblivion, so many things that we need to peel away, to strip ourselves of, in order to get back to the core... so we can rise again in the goodness of every day in balance. The spiral goes up and the spiral goes down... it is up to you which way you take your mind and hence your lives.

If you really need to rant, then set a timer... for one minute, then let it out quick like a pressure cooker valve but see it being turned into rain, into goodness to water the growth of beautiful flowers for your inner garden, your good seeds and then forget it as if you have burnt it up... purify it in the inner white flame, for it is better to do that and let go, than create a big stew that is on the boil for hours or maybe even days. Make the phone call but with a different attitude, of knowing that they will be helpful, so do not go in all gun hoe... for all you will meet with is resistance.

Listen to what you tell yourself. As otherwise it can keep getting worse, what story are you telling yourself and the universe. For as within as without. Grasp this and you will 'know' a miracle for sure and then you will start to believe more and more, you will see the truth until it feels like you are in full control... because really you are! A contradiction that seems again as I say let go... but it takes a while to learn new instructions and for you to be ready, really ready to be back at the helm.

For we would not give a two-year-old a high-end sports car, as they do not know how to use it... drive it and anyway, they couldn't see where they were going with it. So also be sure you 'know thyself well' and be clear about what it is that you truly want... for remember once grasped... you might just get it. How many years have you talked to yourself in the same way and followed the same path? 30, 40, 60 or more? But it is never too late to turn around and change your attitude. I really want you to get this because I probably want it more for you, than what you do for yourselves… in this very moment as I so hate to see you suffering.

Honestly If I can do this, then so can you, for I am just human exactly the same… it does work but we have to feel it, see it and believe it, then it drops to earth. I have experimented with this many times and I know when I doubt I get a sinking feeling but when I am truly keeping the energy at the right positive vibration, then it feels like it is building… building up and moving higher in the body, until it is up in the heart chakra. The love centre, the Christ realized centre and the heart often thuds… for it speaks if you listen and confirms you have been heard, so have faith and trust that your prayer is already answered. The tingling throughout the body is the flow… so feel it and bring it up higher if you can and then see it in the brow, as you then let the feeling explode out… allow the good thoughts to shoot out like a firework into the universe.

Also if you have ever read, which is one of my favourite books called Think and Grow Rich by Napoleon Hill… it speaks of the mastermind and I have often sat at my mastermind table with people of my choice; who I know if they were here on earth, they could help me find the solution. So I go to them and sit down, to tell them what I need in mediation. I place many people at my table including Jesus, for he is in my heart and he knows the truth of what I need. It is like having a case conference for your life and suddenly a day or so later sometimes more, sometimes less you will suddenly see something a different way… a light bulb moment maybe, but something will occur. Napoleon Hill sits next to my spiritual books, including the Bible for all is in balance, as we are part of The One Road.

Remember the lesson I had before with my daughter… The cycle of a repeat? She rang in lack then I flipped, I went in the downward spiral, then my son, then my ex-husband, we were all flipping like dominoes into lack and going down the plug hole, like dirty dishwater. The only thing we can do at any moment is to take responsibility for our own emotions, for we will take ourselves down into the spiral and then pull in everyone around us, instead of going up! So much Love and Light, Peace and Blessings I am sending to you all tonight, for I want this, I want this now so badly for you too but you have to want it for yourself, for only you can do it.

Big hugs XXX

Good Night and God Bless and may the God-Ness of the day stay with you. The universe is a friend, no matter the appearances.

Always X

DAY 32

Good Morning and may the God-ness of the day stay with you.

It has started off well with the news that my old cottage has come back up for rent, so this will be home again for a while. I used to love it there as the grounds were so beautiful, 5 acres and the landlords so friendly.

The universe is working in my favour as I will not accept anything less now and the future is bright, it all comes round again in the hands of time. The cottage, the big house, both of which I have lived in over the years in the same grounds, the place where my father was laid to rest. The memories are both good and sad, as also the place of my divorce.

Yet here we are now friends, even able to share a home if necessary, that is the progress of the unconditional sort. And also though our marriage was lost along the way, other things were discovered. We shall not go back to that, because now for our lives are beyond different but I am so pleased that the future will bring happy, healthy memories. We did use to love the barbecues, the games of badminton and football, picnics with friends and all the fun…so it will be again, for I will make sure of it.

As we have a grandchild now as she too grows, she needs to learn the value of unconditional love. I have arranged to take her to the animal farm on my finish here, so a day with the family will help me to adjust, back into the pace of the world. The day I found my house up north, the 4 bedroom one, all en suite in 5 acres… who would have known what changes would unfold so dramatically, as to look now and see it as it is, just unrecognisable.

I would not have believed anyone who had ever told me this, I would have said you are mad that I would be divorced, my father passed on and that I would be living such a different life of devotion in service. Nothing would have prepared me… anything, for the road is arduous yet at the same time so full of richness, for once you are on you can never get off. Not this one anyway, the real path of Love and Peace.

I have tried to quit many times, for I have not felt strong enough in my fear and lack of faith in my ego. I have like a child stomped my feet and said, "That's it. No more" once or twice. I have been left alone for a day or two but then the longing returns and it is hopeless… so you give up. You eventually give up fighting, you have to or the pain returns, so best to surrender to the greatest power of all within, the greatest Love.

When my last trip to Essex was planned, I did not have the slightest idea about this 40 days of silence and as I stayed in my Shamanic Teachers caravan, they said you are going to lead something. It felt important to do an Ascended Master Mediation prior to my departure and it was during this I saw it, so plain… for the heart was calling me so strong, it reduced me to tears for I was not sure where to go or how this could occur… all I knew was I was not allowed to return home.

All of a sudden, the Garden Station is flashed through my mind and I thought all I can do is ask the question… and within a day it was all set to go, my 40 days and nights within the shed in the woods. For they honoured my calling… Even now, as I write this, it is like a dream for looking back, I remember contacting a friend to tell them with urgency about the next step.

For the next step had been shown and I had no fear, for I knew it, I could feel it, it was like being taken to such a special place of love and I knew it would change me forever and that I would follow it. This book appeared and then the principles, it is like it was waiting to be poured out of a jug… that had been tipping slowly… getting ready to flow in full.

Never again will I mistrust… or lose faith or doubt, for now I can see the way so clearly, it is mine. For if everything goes… then everything arrives, always. The future is going to be different and who knows what else is in store but an adventure is still a welcome surprise and freedom galore. John, I hope you are as proud of me as I was proud of you, undone day, the day I return to you in God's love, we will have so much to talk about. You have not gone far, I know that as you are here to guide me but to see you truly will be wonderful… The evening comes and as I settle for bed, I think over my life in this little shed. How rich am I still… I feel… for nothing surpasses.

This is the most real thing I have ever done in my entire life. Travelling to America alone, Croatia and Italy were all amazing but this… this little shed has been the best of all. As I send out prayers far and wide, one day the world will be a better place as we all join together like the dots in the universe. A yellow Rosebush, a sign of devotion that is what I shall do, plant one here, for in their special place I have found you. Love from the heart always.

Goodnight and God Bless and may the God-Ness of the day stay with you. The universe is a friend.

Always X.

DAY 33

Good Morning and may the God-ness of the day stay with you. The universe is a friend.

Today the frost has returned and it is bitterly cold, like winter has arrived again. So changeable is the weather and I cannot get warm. This aggravates the lingering cough and as my body shakes, I think I cannot stand it. For I am a weakling in the extremes… too cold or too hot, for now I love the balance of all kinds. The middle road of peace… that is for me.

The more I think about it, the more appealing living abroad becomes, especially in the winters. The summers here I love, for England is a country like no other, so green and lush, so many fragrances of flowers and sights to see, coastal paths and castles.

An English man's country is his home… and this I see for it is truly beautiful. Yes, I have appreciated the sights of other countries too and the warmth of the sun as it shines, to be able to witness families still the same, the world over and their sights, their history, their making. I laugh as I think about the friends I have made in Italy and Croatia, for the ladies of the households appear to be the ones who make the plans and the men follow. No different there then. The little gifts, the hugs, the smiles, all the same as here, for friendship in the truth, in the heart is the same everywhere.

As I leave each time, tears are shed for we have become like family… I was thinking the other day if I continue to love this way, my family will be massive. For love, the connection is all there is and I extend it to all who are open to welcome me. The day is slow, for the cold is biting but some trail through, for hot tea, coffee and cake. A man takes photographs, for this is his first time here and I can see by his face that he has made a discovery.

So much is here if people were to come along, more than they think. For not only will you see the garden and its woods, its trails and its space but you will also discover yourself if you stay awhile… and mix with us.

For the good seeds are planted and the old weeds removed, as people change and grow. I can see it happening already, right before my very eyes. Everyone here has been affected in some way, for the positive. The young girls are growing in their confidence, I see them smile and begin to see… we are different. The chatter from the customers and others who stay longer. They wonder what it is… that they can feel but as they return and explore more, it will become clear. The children, the family and the owners are all changed for huge shifts have taken place. They are beginning to shine again from the inside.

Me too, for they have lifted me at times when I have needed it… the support, the friendship, the encouragement as they have watched my tears, my fears and my joy. They root for me like any family would for their blood in unconditional love. We shall miss you they say but I am not going far for I cannot stray, not yet, for this place is wedged in my heart to stay awhile.

Come to Assisi I say, let me show you the sights, the people and the places, for you will surely feel its delight. You are open for change and there is much ahead, as the air of peace and love is in the breath and you have started every day to sit and breathe.

Well done, I say as I too encourage you and root for your development. As I can see the shining eyes and the flicker of the light. The excitement starts to fill the energy fields around you and the seeing begins…

Goodnight and God Bless and may the God-Ness of the day stay with you. The universe is a friend.

Always X.

DAY 34

Good morning and may the God-ness of the day be with you. The universe is a friend.

I awake and immediately think about my trip into town as I need provisions, for each and every time I am trying to avoid human contact, it appears to stalk me as everywhere I go now people say hello.

Lol, there was a time I would have craved company but not so much now, for the feeling has left me. I still love people, do not get me wrong but it's funny how I have changed so much so dramatically inside, not on the outer perhaps. Although some will say so for the outer is reflecting the inner... the peace that comes inside, the loss of attachment... the light for it all shines through in one way or another, for it cannot be hidden. I go for a walk and meditate to connect... really deeply, for I need to stay in my own space today. The day will be long and many will pass by, will they be energy seekers or sharers... I place a golden bubble around me before I leave and ensure that Love can only get in and out, for I wish no one anything but the best. My grandchild is happy... happy as always to see me as I pop in and care for her for a while, as her father is drowning in work. We go to the park where she loves to play and see the water, for she loves the sounds as much as I do and the birds that flit here and there.

Hello, she says all the time, as she expects them to know her and that she will not harm them. The pigeons, the blackbirds, the crows and the chaffinch, she does not care as all she wants to do is love them, to hold them close and to care for them in their beauty, as it is reflected in hers. I have decided to go to an animal farm on the 41st

213

day, to help ground me in a public place, where there will be many. As my introduction back into the world will be harder than I thought. A farm with a grandchild and her parents too, a place where I can see families, interacting, happy in their day out will probably be best, as I need the connectedness with humanity and nature at its best.

Shops and busy places I will have to steer clear of for a while, for the noise perturbs me… maybe short trips in and out to desensitise for a while. I need to hold my space for longer each time and eventually, I can mix again without the drain, or the pain of others suffering. 'Pray' I hear… as each time you leave, you can come back of course, I think I can adjust myself minute by minute and then when home, I can sink myself into my space within… fully immersed and clear my energy field. After she is returned home and my son is finished I decide to go for a walk alone, so back to the park as I link with the flowers, the grass, the trees and the birds.

I move around the park from bench to bench and it must look peculiar, for I sit for a few minutes at each taking stock of the view and breathing it all in.

For you see, the park looks different from different places, just as our perceptions do. From down below, or in the middle, or up high, I can see so many different things from each one, from different perspectives. The park may not move an inch, just as a problem may not but our perspective on it can, at any time. Space can open up, or space can close down, depending upon your free will. You get to choose what you see and what action you take, that is quite empowering really, but many will not recognise it, not yet. For I have been there too, in focus but too much in black and white, when really there was colour but I must have been colour blind to many things and especially to another. Years ago, excuse the pun but I remember hearing, he is so full of s***... his eyes will turn brown. That is no disrespect at all to anyone with brown eyes, for they are truly beautiful, the colour of the earth and I love them. I love them... all the brown, the blue, the green, all as beautiful as the soul that is reflected within them.

I just remember these words for he was full of lies. Not only to himself and to his family but to all around, who he chose to harm, it appeared with intention. A true life liar, such a shame for he believed them all and I now wonder if he is still the same? I must have lied to myself though, many times but certainly not with intention, so I suppose we do not know the reasons behind others actions, for they could be part of a greater plan or a lesson for us.

For the soul signature I know is true... it is not a liar. So best not to judge, Tracy ever... and I wish them well. Suddenly, as I sit quietly in the park I feel a rush of something and it brings me to tears as I can no longer stop it, the feeling comes up and out, regardless it does not care where I am for it is wanting release, so I watch it... as it leaves me. So many times I have felt this pain and I still query... is it mine? I am not thinking about anything at all... Swami comes back to mind for it could be in the consciousness he says, so do not own it, so I choose not to and it soon passes. Later that evening, as I meditate, I realise something, for I have truly linked into my soul's calling. I am Love and I am loved is the feeling, the loneliness has gone for it has disappeared, as I am truly happy with myself and all that I am.

Also the longing... the searching I feel as though it is over? How peculiar for I do not remember any sudden happening? When did that happen I wonder? For has it been a gradual process coming on over the years or has it been this 40 days of going within to finally 'Know Thyself Well' it has certainly done something!

Goodnight and God Bless and may the God-Ness of the day stay with you. The universe is a friend.

Always X.

DAY 35

Good Morning and may the God-ness of the day be with you. The Universe is a friend.

As I awake to the Dawn Chorus, the vibrations are starting already and give me no rest, so it reduces me to tears... How much longer will this continue I think, as the pain increases in velocity? Just as I think the longing has ceased, it begins again... maybe this will be here with me present until the day I am no more, not on earth anyway.

I pray and pray again, am I not a good student, do I not do all I can, to follow the path of truth. I reach despair so many times, and so many times this pain returns and gains in strength... it is unbearable yet not, as somehow I know to carry on in trust and faith as I believe.

It is reducing me to a point where I cannot think at all, the mind will not put anything together, it feels blank and I am unable to focus on anything, except the vibrations which rage through me as they disturb me so much.

The heart starts to pound as I feel into the movement within and breathe slowly... .as I realise the Divine is felt, as it tries to break through taking me over, and forcing me into the flow of pure love so that I cannot attach to anything, not even nature.

As I realise this thought, the purest of love sweeps through me for I am like a rushing river of water in the universal flow of life... I am just a speck, a particle of the stars nothing in matter, for nothing exists except for this... I step outside breathing in the freshness of the morning air, as I try to connect to the earth, to stabilise the energy and allow myself to walk for I am trembling.

I am trembling not only in the strength of the vibrations, but in the sudden magnitude of the realisation that not even nature is a part of me.

All things have to be renounced, all things... even nature for when I live in a world surrounded by beauty I cannot attach, for the external is still external... the plants, the animals all of it, no matter how wonderful they are... they are a representation of the creator as we are... but they are not the Divine Energy, that is now running so rapidly through me.

I go hot and cold and sit for a while as the nature that surrounds me helps the grounding to take place... Dear Lord I pray How can I manifest Heaven on Earth if I cannot connect? To anything at all. How?

There must be a way, a way of the internal becoming the external, as the merging of the two through the heart of grace takes place, for I know I am on the thread... the thread of God's Love and it is bountiful in every way, for I am never separate and never forsaken.

The tears well and flow down my cheeks for this sobbing that occurs so frequently now, is taking me deeper and deeper into a cave of the darkest hours, the dark night of the soul, yet the purest love is rising forth pouring like an overflowing chasm of water... as hot flashes also occur in the burning fire energy... as it is releasing anything that no longer serves me.

Can the physical take this? A fleeting thought passes through my mind but then as I remember the message. 'You will not be given anything that you cannot handle' so I accept and believe that it is right.

Shall I try to stop it? I laugh… for I know that I cannot, no matter what occurs around me for it does not matter what suffering I endure, what I am subjected to, the love has been felt and can never be extinguished, not now…

It is hopeless… I have nothing to do but accept and surrender, always surrender to something far greater than that of any man, woman or beast but trust that all will be taken care of… I believe… I believe becomes my chant.

All of the world's desires rush through my mind as it tries to hang onto something…but as I gently and firmly push it to one side in the acceptance of surrender, I release… through my own heart, in the heart of God's love dissolving the suffering through this beautiful space.

I melt away the pain in the arms of the beloved, as such is the love that cannot be spoken for it is a silence so deep, so tranquil, so still that it is heard… by the soul.

The day unfolds and as I wander the woods, I see the landscape through another lens, this time with a clearer, less blurred focus, as the picture of the world before me is like a painting, a beautiful landscape full of colour yet almost translucent… it is as if I could place my hand upon it and brush it away… Is it a thought in my mind I wonder… my energy field around me as nothing is real, am I like the person in the film... the field of dreams creating my own reality?

Can I be like the magician and shift the illusion at anytime, as I let the thought go and allow the universe to become mine, in a state of acceptance that there is something greater.

Molecules all tightly packed together... solid, gas and liquid...hmm a realisation occurs as I feel into the space of knowing I can create anything in the heart of grace... so I must choose to live in a calm and positive state, as the energy will flow regardless in whatever thoughts I have so they may as well be beneficial ones?

The universe will pick up my thoughts and as they drift upon the energy fields within this land of love imagine? What good could be done... so much!

Tonight I can feel my family members passing by, in the consciousness... an omen is there, and something is going to occur? As they often pop by when a change is imminent.

I feel into the energy and it is lovely to feel their presence and know I am not alone ever... in any way, I know this as I am not separate from the whole but it is good to feel their energy too linked into the pool of eternal love.

First my mum, then my dad, my Nan and then my grandfather (pap) as we used to call him... the love I felt as a child, I shall never forget it, just the best form of human love as I was so blessed to have had this experience in my lifetime.

Are the extended relatives ok? I must ring them when I am out of the 40 days silence, as one never knows just how much time we have left to share together in this world and I love them too so much; for they are a special part of this world…

As I listen to the nothingness of the nature, only its sounds the creak of the trees, the birds.

The woodpecker is loud today… as he drills away so disciplined is he, as he searches for his food, he never stops until he has completed his task, maybe this is an example for us all to see how he focuses on his goal… never give up… Tracy never for you have got this.

It is time for bed and I am in need of sleep, I am hoping I will dream tonight as the end of my silence is near heading to where, I wonder?

The sound of the owl hooting is heard and the birds evening song…I shall miss this, all of it…my goodness this really has become my home, this shed who would have thought it… I am so very grateful.

Goodnight and God Bless and may the God-ness of the day stay with you.

The Universe is a friend.

Always X

DAY 36

Good Morning and may the God-Ness of the day be with you. The universe is a friend.

I awake at Dawn Chorus and listen to the noise outside, I can hear the birds and people already pulling up in their cars, they are starting to move around and this causes a feeling of frustration. Lying in my bed, wondering if I should move but I feel drawn to stay, to stay where I am, yet I feel compelled. Not again… my thoughts are linking into the consciousness of others, so I step back and go back to rest. Tea and toast with the curtains open and as I step outside, I see a woman surprised to see me emerge from a shed in a dressing gown. She stares as I stare back but I think, oh well she has seen me now, so what.

As I continue to get ready for the day and wonder which path she has taken, for she must be on a walk in the woods. No dog was to be seen, she looked alone, so maybe she too needs to be within her own thoughts. Her energy I can still feel, as this is my quiet place, so funny really, for now I am like the dog in my territory. The woods I do not own, so let her be… the thought fleets in, as she may need this beautiful energy and it could be helping her in some way. The earth does not belong to any man, not really anyway, no matter what is stated upon your deeds, for one day you will be gone and it will be left behind.

Share and share alike Tracy, something that you are usually very good at. Later I decide to walk down into the village and her car is still there, so she must have gone far… I am now hoping she is okay and enjoying the view. I decide to take the public path and wander through the trees until I reach the roadside, I see no one. The stream is noisy and the cars more but the beauty is so wonderful, for I see much that cannot be seen from inside any transport. Even the cyclists concentrate on their cycling, they miss it all too... and they are surprised to see me.

Some nod and say hello others just stare, for has walking gone out of fashion, in our fast-paced world? Each corner I turn, new sights are shown and eventually I come across a castle, so I venture inside for coffee. For I am free... free to be me and do whatever I please. As I sit upon a window seat to rest, the castle in all its glory beckons me, so I link into its walls and its history.

Such a beautiful hall, so steeped in music and dance as I gaze out of the window into the grounds. The sound of music fills my ears, the birds too as they join in and then the smells remind me of faraway places, as the fragrance fills my nose.

I am transported back in memory to a place with walls of solid stone, with a fire glowing in the corner. Chatting with a friend and then another place, a tall tower looking all over the town. The belfry, as I turn and catch a glimpse of him taking my picture. The love rises suddenly in flow through my body and fills the heart, with both the bittersweet taste of love and sorrow together. Do not attach but let it be... I think as it rests within the Memory of a good place, the past is gone, so do not be in sorrow for 'We are not our story' and you enjoyed it all then and will again. It may not be the same place or the same people, but It will be there once more, for you know the truth of it all now and so does God.

The sun is shining today and it warms my skin, my face and crown of my head, as I walk back down the lane. Further along, I stop for a car to pass and look to the left as a stream is rushing down like a waterfall, rumbling over steps of rock as if cut out by hand, so beautiful a sight and not one seen by the busy traveler zipping by. I am so blessed.

A badger, a pheasant, a rabbit all killed by the road, for humankind has invaded their home. Plastics, paper cups, McDonald's boxes, even a flask... why? Why throw these out of your windows when you could surely take them home?

A little inconvenience in what has become an instant gratification and throw it out trash world. The animals will choke and suffocate upon them and if I had a sack or two I would definitely fill them, for it is everywhere in the bushes, off the track, in the stream, hanging over branches, think before you throw it out for you are destroying our planet. As I walk further down, a small sign points to another off-road space, a track leading back up into the woods is found, so I explore it further and such a sight is a delight to my shining eyes.

A really old bridge over the stream and the sun glistening through the gaps, so I decide to stop and eat my lunch, whilst I meditate and pray here for a moment in the wilderness. My sandwich is eaten, along with juicy cherry tomatoes, the flavour and they appear to taste better than what I thought they could. As I carefully fold up the foil and place it back in my backpack, ready for a bin.

To stay here would be just magical...this place another home in the making for sure. For if I were homeless, this is where I could live. My imagination starts to play... What about a paddock nearby with a tent or a shed? Lol, I think I can live anywhere now, for I am internally happy. On my return the owner is near and we chat as something pops up and I lose my track, my track... as I start to justify.

But I quickly stop and turn myself around, for nothing can justify my own behaviour, so I take responsibility for all I have been, done and said... Nothing can justify, unless someone has a knife to my child's throat, for then surely I can defend. But if another adult is colour blind and cannot see green, then I have to remember that and keep to my own path. For nothing justifies my 'reaction' and hurting the feelings of another, nothing. My only saving grace is that it was never with intention and God knows the truth and what is in my heart always. Every day is a good day... do you know that Tracy, for there is always something achieved, learnt or lost as we let go of all attachments.

As I sat in meditation, I received a message like a light bulb, as it dropped from above, plop into my head, from nowhere. Sew up your pockets... the universe said... sew them up both of them, for now at least you need to hold it all. Just remember to distribute and then let go... for you will return with nothing. The tears softly fall as my heart explodes, with the feeling of the message. Thank you I say in gratitude, for now I am receiving all that I like to give and share out in the world, for I realise that nothing is permanent here on earth, as it stays in the illusion. 'Heaven on Earth' though I can see and many too will benefit, for when the heart is open wide, in both truth and love, without ego faith appears.

God knows for it is 'felt' in him, in the Christ Consciousness not shown and he will recompense. The good... are sometimes not what they seem but neither are bad, so do not judge, how can we... not unless we want to be judged ourselves. A fine line is always trodden... 'Know Thyself Well'. Listen to your thoughts, Tracy I remember well, what comes out your mouth and always watch your own behaviours, for what Archetype could you be standing in? The Mother, The Father, The Child, The Warrior, The Lover, or even

Lucifer… we are all responsible, as we are all born whole with the curse or the blessing whatever is your perception of free will. The 'I' has puzzled me today for in the ego it can reign supreme but then again, God says I Am I am the way, the truth and the life.

I am that I am, I am all that I am, and so I now feel it is perception and intention that is the cause of many misunderstandings. As long as your intention is clear with respect to all, then I am happy for the I to remain in love. Today has been a mindful day in nature and so assuring that it is here for us all to discover when we are ready. At 8.00 the bed beckons and I receive a message, an instruction to sleep only on the mattress on the floor… I wonder why that is? But instead of doubt I immediately follow instruction for a faithful student trusts in love.

As I lie down, my body aches a little from all the walking, immediately the waves begin to flow up and down, up and down the physical. I relax into the mattress and notice my body is straight; perhaps I am usually blocking something in the softness of the bed. I fall into the waves and gently the slumber begins, as I awake now and again with a noticing.

My arms are above my head again and my hands are together as if bound… not a position I remember ever laying in, the waves are still there but gentle not throwing me around, so I relax some more and off I start to go into dreams.

Good Night and God bless for today has been a wonderful day, and may the God-ness of the day stay with you. The universe is a friend.

Always. X

DAY 37

Good Morning and may the God-ness of the day be with you. The universe is a friend.

This morning I awake with the sound of a pheasant at the bowl outside my window, he is screeching and competing with the others for the last crusts of the bread. I fall back off to sleep, for my body is still in need of rest as this cough has nearly cleared but it is still here on and off, so I relax and listen. The time is now 8.00... gosh that was a long sleep but I must have needed it for the physical awakes when it is ready. Immediately I can feel the depth of the love within and a realisation occurs... I Am Love... I really am.

Not the playing of the archetype, or the idea of but the very being of Love as I can feel it so deeply, like a deep, deep current that is running within the soul. I remember waking up with certain waves during the night and the body jerking as someone was linking in with curiosity. I Am Love... I remind myself, for no one can take away my authenticity, not now, for 'I Know myself Well.'

These 40 days has cleared a lot and helped me to see even more, so I shall stay true to myself now, forevermore. I am emotional as it is nearly time for me to leave here and still, I cannot think even if I wanted to, so I trust that the right people are in place at the right time and for the right reasons and that the steps are here.

The owner contacted me the other day, for out of the blue a local radio station has been in touch and she knew. She knew to tell them about my 40 days, my journey and the insights gained, so she is coming here to see me, for she needs to know more. This morning I switch on quick to check on my daughter as she has been very ill and there was a message flashing from a book publishing company who I sent my first book manuscript to. She said when I can call? So I can discuss with you how to take your book to the next level. But as I link to her message, I wonder if she has even read it, for there is no feeling in her reply. I have not replied as yet, for I want to see what substance she is made of, for my book was written from the heart and here to help many.

The second one will be ready soon, I think as I would like it to reach all over the continents, to help many, as many that can be, to begin to 'Know Thyself Well'. For if nothing else if I light a spark, a tiny spark of love in one... then my mission will be complete. For if one tells one, that makes two... Then two tell one and that makes 4 and eventually the good seeds are planted for all, as we join together like dots in the consciousness of Love. Real love... the kind within us all. A walk was taken this evening just before dinner and I decided to go up higher, as I reach the top I can see a way forward, so I stop for now as I have forgotten my wellingtons.

I shall return tomorrow and bring a picnic, for this will be a good one to follow. I walk behind a pheasant on my return, a good luck sign and he does not see or hear me, as I am walking mindfully. It is only when he finally turns around that he screeches and soars away in fear, for I am too near for his liking. Funny I thought just like people sometimes, for when we open ourselves up to real love they slam the door shut, for they are scared to receive... As I reach the bottom, I sit for a while next to the fountain and as a gaze at the earth, it starts to heave... Up and down it rises like it is breathing again and I see a shift in something. As it is happening instead of trying to figure it out, I let it go in complete trust that is all is well. Usually, I get these occurrences after a walk in a Labyrinth, but this must be because I have connected to nature. As I was walking mindfully through the woods, the trees, the fields, for it is having the same effect on me. As the evening progresses, for the first time I have the feeling to be out in the world, with a sense of urgency... as though I am needed to speak my truth and be visible, in my authenticity. I have not felt this before but as I look in my diary only three more days, how strange for I am happy, really happy in my little home, my shed, my place of peace and tranquility.

There is no anxiety about the future... none, for it does not matter as I will be lead, just as I will help anyone who is looking for their special place within. In fact, the future feels exciting, I have sewn up my pockets and I am ready, ready for whatever comes before me. Dinner is enjoyed outside and it is delicious... for I make a Vegetarian Bolognese with mushrooms, onion and tomatoes and strawberries and cream for dessert. I feel a bit nauseous, as my eating habits have changed too and now portion sizes are smaller with no snacks in between, so that is quite a lot of food.

That is a change for me... because I have been an emotional eater and could normally eat you out of house and home. But it appears the more you begin to connect within, the less you crave, as the happier you are and I am happy. I am still not perfect in any way...even though my nickname is Mary Poppins. Lol, but I am releasing it all as it comes into my awareness and allowing the good seeds to grow.

Occasionally, the shadow rears its head but I put it in its place, for fear or anger never gets you anywhere but perhaps dead or worse still on a cycle of repeat. I will state my facts and tell you straight but I will not chew the fat...what a waste of energy is that. Let's get together and have a ball... as many hands make light work but if you are not interested then just stay out my way and that is all for we are each to our own path. If you would like my help in any way and I can, then it is here, as my door is always open in Love.

You are welcome, as I have said before if you want to come, come but come in Peace with an open heart. I may pose a question and ask you what it is that you want, as an archetype may be at play but if you leave them at the door like your shoes and come inside in your authenticity like I will to you; then you cannot lose. For you will be forever welcome in my house, for evermore... I keep getting a message drop in not to forget about the six-pointed star? Which one is that again, I need to look it up. The star of David and the two inverted triangles representing 'heaven on earth' not a war between countries. Also signs of the spirit and the realms... some people are frightened of these but not to be, for only the 'good' is allowed.

I will never listen to anything or anyone that says about harming for that is not the truth of the Lord or any prophet. Mischief makers and misguided ones pass back from this life as they have not learnt and it takes time for them to grow and to evolve. So only goodness please, remember that as in all the doctrines and in science, astrology and the tales the myths, the truth is there in the common thread, for us all to work together in peace, as we are all as ONE.

Each human has dreams, some a family, children, a home, they are a brother, a sister, a mother, a father, a wife, a husband, a grandparent, an aunt, an uncle, a cousin...we are all connected!

Have you ever thought about doing your DNA strand... you could be surprised by where you have originated from? So do not hate anyone, for back in time if traced through history, they could have been your direct family... do not pass judgement, unless you want it in return. Remember our soul signature is not a colour or a creed or a belief, or anything of the sort for we are all as ONE. Show me that your soul is a different colour to mine? Impossible for it cannot be… you are the same as me and me as you.

Let us look deep into each other's eyes and be honest as we get to 'Know Thyself Well'. Fear is usually at the base of all things negative and misinformation… I remember my 5-year old coming home from school, only been attending for less than a year and I realised she was racist, for she was discriminating against black children.

For as I asked her about her day, she told me she had been paired up in the dinner line with a little girl but she would not hold her hand because it was dirty. What do you mean dirty, I asked? And as she explained, I was heartbroken for both of them, the little children so innocent and already the world has taken its toll on them both. So I explained about the colours of the skin but that we are all the same inside but I could see from her expression that she was not accepting of this.

So the following day I went to town and bought her a black doll for her pram. Oh dear, it was terrible the way she treated this doll, so different from the rest. For she was neglected, not dressed in the pretty fine clothes and sat with the rest. She was isolated from the group, she did not join in the teas but she was outcast, to sit alone naked. Each time I brought her back into the fold, redressed… and each time she was discarded until in the end, my daughter grew angry at my actions and threw her out!! Omg, what was I to do? For she was only 5 years old. So when I speak with her again and again, re-educating the mind, giving her new information in so many different ways, until one day she said on return home from school, 'I played with Diane today!' I praised her so much for she was breaking through the barrier, I like her she said... thank goodness I thought, so invite her for tea, I replied, and she did.

But then she was the one who was hurt! For the family would not allow it... they would not allow their daughter to come for tea. I felt they were afraid, afraid of discrimination and of their daughter ending up being hurt in some way by us. So when my daughter felt the pain of racism in a way returned it taught her well, for then and only then did she truly understand her actions. 'Reap what you sow'. I am pleased to say they stayed friends at school and now as years have passed, many boyfriends passed through the door of different persuasions, for she has an open heart as she has learnt her lesson and learnt it well.

An open door was always my philosophy, for we come from the same source and return home together as one. In later years, a hospital trip became necessary and as I took her to A and E later, a doctor came out to see us with her blood test results. He looked at me with a 'twinkle' in his eye and said, did you have an affair with a man of the med? What, I said... no of course not! With that, he explained my daughter's blood is rare and carrying something called Non-Thalassemia, as her cells are shaped differently to others, and that is usually only found in Africa or the Mediterranean.

I panicked, would she be ok I asked, yes he said but she should carry a card, just in case she ever needs a transfusion. For had it been full blown Thalassemia, she would have needed regular transfusions her entire life, then my mind was confused for she has been taken to special care not long after birth, had they mixed up the babies I thought? No he said, it is just because it is rare. It is a genetic time jump down the line, like two white people suddenly having a black baby out of nowhere. The more I thought about it she was different to the rest, as they placed her in my arms I had noticed it, for the others were born with fine blonde hair and blue eyes and she was born with olive skin and hair so dark as it wrapped around her head, so thick and beautiful. It was like she was born having been to the hairdressers. She looked like a little Indian... a guru at birth, for how we commented on it, how funny we said, as we both then laughed.

Honestly how many rare things can we get I said, as we already have another with Cystic Fibrosis and that is genetic too and can come out at any time. If two meet with the same gene, a million one chance that doctor said. So you see the DNA blood test would be interesting, for down the line we must have travelled far and wide and married others from different cultures, how wonderful as rich a tapestry this world is!! Quite amazing... for little did my daughter know she was from another heritage.

Good Night and may the God-ness of the day stay with you. The universe is a friend.

Always. X

DAY 38

Good Friday and Full Moon…Good Morning and may the God-ness of the day be with you. The universe is a friend.

3+8 = 11 New Beginnings for sure I can feel it throughout me as the waves have returned during the night, so regular but not too strong, although enough to disturb me. A great fear arose in the night like a clap of thunder it came and I did not fight it, as I allowed to rage through me. This time I completely let go… Because I thought just carry on doing… doing what you will… you cannot harm me at all, for I am safe in the heart of Love.

I had a realisation about my work and how it had been so small, as I looked again at the contents and the small steps that lead to the greater plan. But now the greater plan felt bigger than what I had imagined as I dared to dream big. Has God picked up the plan and ran off with it, I thought in his imagination, for I surely know that if you fill your cup, your space, a bigger one will be given.

How can you fill that though, the fear said? You will… was the response from within, just trust and have faith. Each time I pray now, the tears roll down my cheeks, slowly yet I am not sad or afraid. So it must be the love, the inner Love leaking from my soul, for it so resonates with its own beauty, its wisdom, its understanding and its connection, for they are truly sacred. This morning it is a beautiful day and I try to capture the photograph of this place, to keep it in my memory for it is sketched in my heart and I want to savour it all, for it is nearly time.

Three more sleeps… like the children used to say in great excitement before Xmas. The final countdown, only this brings me back to tears for once gone, it will be no more sleeps here for me. I love this place, for so special it has become, magical woodland and garden, still in its creation, yet my inner garden has grown, it has blossomed like no other and has become full... full of creativity and love.

The dew is on the chair outside, the mist begins to rise, and the sun shines on the left, creating pockets of shadows. While the mist hangs between the trees on the right. The flowers are all so colourful, the bushes and the blossoms and the birds, they sing away with all their might. I shall never forget this. For how can I, it is as much a part of me, as I am a part of it, in the one universe, the connection with God's creation for us all as we join the dots. Last night, I arose as bodily functions demanded and as I stepped outside it took my breath away for in the silence, the stillness of the night I could see the moon shining between the trees, the sun, the orange still glistened slightly behind it in alignment and it was glorious. As I stood and stared, it was magical, the energy I could feel, as nearly a full moon.

It was as if it spoke, for it was as large as life and the hum of its vibration reached my heart so deep, I cried. The balance of the world in the dark and the light.

The beauty still so vibrant, many animals roaming around hidden but there, another version of the world alive and operating under the same laws like the one we see in the daylight, the perfect balance of peace. I am getting ready to go out on a little adventure today, I shall pack a picnic and off into the wilderness to see what I can find if anything. I keep hearing things, these past few days, just subtle noises of animals nearby, yet I cannot see them.

235

My senses must have heightened in the silence, for I keep turning and looking, thinking that I am going to see someone or something but nothing is there for they are too quick.

My little emergency sewing kit that I remembered to bring, has assisted me in sewing my pockets up and I am so pleased for now I can place my odd gloves within them for my walk. I did have a pink pair and a grey pair but like socks that disappear, they too have wandered off, so I am left with one of each. So what, it does not matter, does it?

If I am not colour coordinated...

Lol, I can almost hear some say... Oh No, I could not have that! As such importance is placed upon such things of nonsense, in today's world.

The poorest I feel in other countries are sometimes the richest, for they appear to discover their inner love, their spiritual gifts far quicker than us in the west and we think we are the most civilised.

I take my picnic and go up into the hills until I find a log on which to sit and just soak in the view over the valley. It is hot... like a summer day, as I eat my sandwich and my mind drifts away... to the days of Scotland. I shall return I am sure for it feels like another adventure, maybe I should have moved there before or at least visited again often.

There is so much more to see the coastal islands and beyond, so I will get a tent and see how far I reach, for there is nothing really to stop me, only myself. I wonder if anyone would like to come with me. A few days here and there, to explore and discover the coves that are hidden in the landscape. Nature, the seals, the beaches and more for it is all there.

Good Night and may the God-ness of the day stay with you. The universe is a friend.

Always. X

DAY 39

Good Morning and God Bless and may the God-Ness of the day be with you. The Universe is a friend.

As I awake today with the current of the waves flowing through me, I can hear a song being played in the background; it is a song from Beauty and the Beast. Symbolic I feel to the events that are occurring now in my life.

The realisation through these 40 days of silence that there is more to life, indeed there is and it is there for us all to receive into our hearts once recognised.

Also, it was the full moon last night, as a healing white witch reminded me, a magical moon for transformation. Are two of the Kings on their way I wonder, are they nearby, one in ego and one in disguise. We shall see and will I recognise them? I switch on my phone and then realise as it is a work day and my final sleep here is tomorrow, only two more nights of sleep to go.

Then my phone will be back on again and I am back in the world fully from Easter Monday. I have mixed feelings about this, as my time here has been so precious and my life my own… This feeling I wish to keep forever so I will engage in regular periods of silence. As my connection with the Lord is not to be disturbed and has become my priority. For it keeps me full… full of love and full of life in all its goodness.

Daily meditation and prayer has become the norm and will continue for the rest of my days, I know that now, for it is forever etched in my heart… A voice mail is waiting on my phone, so I listen and hear a lady in suffering waiting for assistance, so I return her call. A lovely conversation was held as she is in need of unconditional love and realises much about herself, she was open honest and transparent about her flaws and that was appreciated as I give her my time. For that is all we need to do, be honest with ourselves and then act upon the clearing of all, the peeling away of the onion for we can truly cultivate our internal garden and allow the good seeds to grow.

Not the easiest thing to do so I admire her courage, as I have been there; and I congratulate her on her achievements thus far. For she is working hard, hard on herself and she will succeed. She decides to come to Drum Circle and listens intently to what else we offer here, she becomes excited about how the universe has drawn her to this place and she knows now she will not be judged. For how can we judge others when we have been through so much ourselves, our lessons, our trials and our tribulations? We cannot, for if we do, we are nowhere near our destination. My daughter rang this morning too and as I mentioned her entry in this book, she laughed because she said for I was only talking about that the other day.

She was explaining how hard it must be in a rural place for a new doctor to assist their patients, especially when from another culture, as judgment could be with immediate effect. She loves her village, the sense of community but it can be hard if people do not go outside of their 5-mile circuit and engage in the world. That so reminds me of my ex-husband when we met for he too was from a village and had not ventured far, so a Coventry City girl was quite an excitement. As later we decide to move to be near to my parents, I laugh as I receive a call. "Where are you?" I said, as he had nipped out to the shops and was getting the bus home to our new flat in Coventry.

I am not sure he said but I think it is in Birmingham! Omg, how on earth did you manage that, you were supposed to get off 18 miles ago, as I am now in hysterics cross the road and get back on a bus to Coventry, I instruct him and then get off at… Over the years I have travelled far and wide to show the children all the places I can, to enable them to experience many aspects of the world at large and all its richness and now I realise it has helped them to become rounded in their view and allow everyone to be unique in their own identity.

What a beautiful day it is today as I sit here writing in the shade for it is hot… so hot like a summers day. Suddenly I hear the woodpecker but I cannot believe it for it sounds like a pneumatic drill… for you never guess he is having a go at the corner of my shed. Lol. It is so loud as he is close, good lord how funny it must look from the outside, as he hammers away, I only hope the shed will hold up for it leans to one side and is full of holes. People are chatting in the gardens and dogs are lying with their owners, the theatre group that is coming has been advertised all around, as the flyers have arrived and life is good. Life can be good every day, I believe that. Perhaps one day in the past I would have said different but not now, for I have grown myself and know who I am in my wholeness and the gifts that I have to share with the world.

Plus as I now say with clarity, we are not our story, we really are not, and once we understand this, it can be the undoing of us the peeling away of what no longer serves us! A lady has just come by to inquire what we do here and as I link to her energy, what a lovely feel she has, for people are being drawn here now, more and more for once we made the decision firmly in our minds, the energy flowed. As we too learnt to receive as well as give and open our hearts… people arrive, as they feel the draw to be near, they want to know more. I am so pleased, so pleased for the owners, for without them I certainly would not be here and you would not be reading this. I cannot praise them enough for they opened their hearts in trust and love and let me in. Now for sure, they are in mine and as I see a message flashing on my phone from down south, when can we come up they say? For they are excited too.

They want to bring their energy up here now so much, as I have previously taken mine down to them. They want to share in all we do and help us on our way, bless them I say for I know they are so beautiful. And people will benefit so much from their presence too. I will ring later I say, as I can feel their hearts explode in love, for they have travelled this journey with me too and need to speak.

A party is about to arrive... I love a celebration! For my father was especially good at these, as we had many over the years. My open house must have stemmed from this, I think as he always made people welcome and the fun we had. I can remember grandparents, aunts and uncles, cousins too, neighbours and all our friends, the Tea Cakes, Sandwiches and Sausage rolls, Cockles and Welsh cakes all styles and types of food. But the most important thing of all was the 'sound', the sound of the peals of laughter, the love that rang through that house, as we enjoyed it all. These special times are here again as I now take the lead and my family too will follow in my footsteps as I help to lead them back into their happiness, their open homes and their hearts in love.

My mother in law, I remember once when my father was older and ill with his paranoia, she said to me don't ever doubt yourself Tracy, for you are full of love, you are a good person. She hugged me tight and held me close, so out of character, for not something that she would normally do but somehow as I looked at the tears in her eyes, her heart had been touched over the years... and we knew each other, in our unconditional love.

For in the early days, she was not that keen on me... lol... for taking her son away but over time she came to see that I loved him and that I would have done anything for him and to support him with a good future. Now we are divorced, it is funny because it is me that she asks to see... or phones, or asks when I am visiting, not me he says! Quite indignant as I get the message from my ex, it's never me she wants, it's always you. Honestly, jealousy it rears its head in so many places... Just be pleased she finally likes me, it's only taken 30 + years, so he laughs instead.

I have to laugh too, for who would have guessed it... You are 'Mrs. Pringle' she says only you. Now... now, don't be silly, I say for he must find someone too, so he is happy and I will be happy for him, as well as you will. As she then pulls that face I know so well, the one that used to be pulled at me, he will be fine I say, just give him time... and don't get in the way!

Just as I am writing this, the song Valerie comes on the radio... I Love you Val, I say always. X

I have always tried hard with my son's partner, for there is nothing worse than not being accepted, as my father was hard on him, for no one would have good enough for his daughter... so she has become like a daughter to me and she has now gifted me the greatest gift of all, our granddaughter. So you see she will always be special, for that is one of the greatest things that anyone could have given in love.

The day progresses well and as all the people leave, it is time for us now, a barbecue they say and as we light a fire in the pit and cook away, how lovely I think to be here. Even though not my direct family, they are in a way to remembering we are all linked... in the one universe.

A beautiful evening and much ado the children are tired as they have been to the beach today, swimming they say and building castles. So much fun.

Do not forget I say, to pop by and see me in the morning for the Easter bunny may have left you something you never know. The little one only three, she looks at me full of expectation... yes, she says I will. These are just the best times... remember them well and etch them in your memories and in your hearts. I look at the flames in the fire as they leap and play and the stars in the sky as we begin to say goodnight, for how blessed am I

As I speak with my shamanic teachers full of love and praise, I smile for they are special, I will be down soon to see you I say as I need to catch up and also have more lessons for I must not stray from my goals and my path.

We are proud of you, they say as we speak about the future and only one more sleep. Tracy they say, you should be proud too for you have done it, really you have, for you walk your walk, not just talk the talk. Ah, thank you. I say in reply for I have heard that before from a friend and I know just how hard it is to do but I will try my best not just for myself but for you all... to lead the way. It is time for bed and as I relax in the shed, I look around with so much love for this place, only one more sleep... one more precious sleep here for me.

Good night and God Bless for may the God-ness of the day stay with you. The Universe is a friend always and as in words and a memory of a very dear friend, God is good.

X

DAY 40

Good Morning, God Bless and may the God-Ness of the day be with you. The universe is a friend.

The final day, how much of a surprise is this, for I cannot believe I have been here for six weeks. The time has flown and the pleasure been great, even amongst the snow, the hail and the wind. I have faced many things and looked deep within as I have sought out my shadow and seen much, the devil dwells within as well as the angel.

Yet somehow I have known how to be at the core… it is there, for if we override our impulse and do not use free will for the ill, we can rise again in goodness as we do not allow fear to become the superior. When faced with a choice, I have had to feel into space and learn to know which one serves my higher self. Remember the message. 'Know Thyself Well'. My daughter rang this morning so very upset and in her distress, I spoke to her in the same way that I talk to myself. But mum she said I want to dance with the devil today, for I feel I would surely go in anger and slay for an episode has occurred and she has had to step right back because she knows in her heart like us all, she could kill especially when hurt.

Stepping back is hard to do, especially when we feel protective of our loved ones but which is the right way? And which will not serve you I say.

I am proud of her, as I hear her anguish, as it tears at her very core and I am proud of her because she recognises how past issues can cause a reaction. A past hurt can fly up to the surface, which then enters the mix and can then cause further problems. Facts only, I said no fiction…no exaggeration only facts, for the law will not operate on any other, not only the law of the land but the law of the universe. The facts are present, she said as there are witnesses, but still I say wait... and see how you feel in a few minutes. As she could be the one to then lose her temper and hurt, if she allows the anger to rise and take over, in her free will. So hard for a mother to do yet, I have to allow them to make their mistakes and their choice, at least she rang. I think to myself and checked herself out with me. No matter what... I say in reply, I have brought you up well and I do not want to see any cycle of repeat, from any other places of influence.

No matter how much I love you, I will not visit you in a prison cell and see your lives ruined. War will not solve war I said, it is like throwing oil on a hot fire, it will explode, so you have to find the best possible way to resolve this. Look at the bigger picture, draw a boundary but also realise there is something wrong here... for they are not behaving in the right way and they could be suffering too and allowing their free will to reign in their own pain.

They do need to learn that actions have consequences and their behaviour has recently escalated... so stop! Relax and think before you act, for there could be something behind this that you are not aware of.

Lessons to learn for all I say and this could be a blessing in disguise, as she needs to stand in her own power and not be afraid ever again but she needs to handle this situation well. Later on, she rings and she has done just that, well done I say for you are setting an example and I am proud of you. I will see you later for tea and give you the biggest of hugs, for I know that you need one and I love you so much. How the devil comes to tempt us as .that could have easily turned the other way and become extremely serious. The threat is still there and if they do not listen and behave accordingly, then the law will have to take over but at least they have done the right things for now, for themselves. Step by step, they are learning and being shown the way the proper way in truth and love for all. Today is warm and the birds are singing. I have walked the woods and fed them all, people are arriving.

A Reiki session is completed and a painful shoulder released, as the person says at the end with a puzzled look, your hands? They are red hot! So many say that I say, as I was worried I would drip on them, for the sweat was pouring off me in the energy.

As they smile and leave so much more relaxed, I think to myself I have the best job in the world! For I love to assist others where I can and see them leave happy. The children are bounding around the garden and I have given them a little gift, just a chocolate egg and a colouring book each but the reward was mine for in their little faces so lit up and grateful. The little one comes back later and says, Tracy... I need to give you a cuddle. Her sweetness eats into my heart, for she is truly beautiful inside and out.

As the day goes on and people come and go all happy as the sun is shining and the families all reminisce together, what a wonderful they say as they are all enjoying the Peace of this beautiful place and the magical energy of the Garden Station.

The children come back again and this time, I read the little one a story... but not from a book, as I open my hands and allow the magic to come forth. She gazes into my palms as if the pages are alight with colour and as I weave her name into the story, it truly comes alive. She opens her hands as she copies me and we enter the forest, together. For in the forest, she meets 'Norman, The Weary

Elf' for he is so busy picking up all the rubbish that the big people always leave behind, that he no longer has the time to go the fairies parties and he is so sad... But our little friend can help and help she does, as she enlists her brother and other friends for they are good and the forest floor is quickly cleared.

It is amazing to watch her little face as she relishes it all and watches with interest as the Elf gets dressed in his Sunday best, ready for the fairy celebrations. For thanks to her, this is the first time in a very long time that he has been able to attend. As her brother then runs over in delight, for he has found some treasure, a hidden egg and shares it with her, for they are both kind and caring children. She looks at the rubbish he has placed upon the table, the golden wrapper and off she runs with it in hand. Where are you going, I ask? As she is only three, just to get rid of the rubbish, she shouts back at me! A little story but a big impact... so much goodness can be woven into the hearts of our children, the next generation if only we open up ours and clean our internal garden. Another walk through the wood for suddenly I can feel a wave, a wave of powerful energy starting to rush through me and I have to bend over to breathe... As I sink in, I recognise this for it has returned, someone is trying to link in with me. And as it builds and builds, I need to either lie down or walk, so I walk hard and fast through the trees until I find my special resting place.

I sit with my back against a tree and the body starts to jerk, as I try not to attach to the energy, for they are thinking of me. Let go, let go I think for this is not serving me and you are seeking my energy. Slowly it ebbs away and I relax again, they do not mean any harm and it is in love they come, but why? Something is occurring, could it be with them? For I can feel it whirring, the universe as it turns but as I remind myself to mind my own business, I let it go again and eventually it subsides.

That is strange I think as that normally happens when they are near, or could it be they are passing by, or resting, for usually at other times they are too distracted by the world. I walk up high onto the bridge and see across the wood, I suddenly feel as though I am being watched, somehow from afar. But they are not here, I know this for I can now feel it but they are 'visioning' and can see, so I decide to send out prayers with so much love, light and compassion, not only to them but to everyone in the world.

Later on, I leave for a few hours and go for tea with my daughter as she has moved into a new home. I arrive and see it is beautiful, exactly right… a little home as if made especially for her.

I am so pleased and look around in delight for it has that feel of a very special place. She will be fine. I think to myself for I can see the bigger picture and she has been given an opportunity now to have her life back. I tell in so many words the feeling I can feel and she confirms, she is truly happy with her decision.
Bless you Alice, for you really deserve this now and the future is looking bright. Well done, for today I remember to say as I hug her tight for she is showing me her maturity and I trust her implicitly for she is on the right road now to discover who she truly is in love.

As I arrive back at the shed, the owner is waiting and as we chat I can see the tears building up in her eyes, I have never felt like this before she says as she clutches her heart. You are family to me, to us she says and remember we are here. If you need to walk away at any time, the door is open. As a heartfelt thank, you are said and hugs are exchanged… I know I shall be present and around for a very long time. I may travel and move around but I will always come home, for home is where the heart is and my heart is both here and down south.

The heart can be anywhere…in this country or abroad, as it is in the links with the people and not just the places. It feels like an epic journey has occurred and many lives have been changed along the way, not just mine for the love ripples out around us all and we are truly blessed. Well, last sleep it is; and I prepare my bed for the last time, I notice the angel appears to have moved on my table and she is now facing the door for I am loved, loved and watched over for evermore.

40 days and 40 nights… in the shed, as I shake my head in wonder. What next! Dear Lord, for this has been the best gift that I have ever been given. I kneel and pray and say thank you from my very core, for without this experience I may never have discovered who Tracy Pringle really is…

Re-entry tomorrow and a certain excitement is beginning, for this really is a new life, rebirth and the start of a whole new world!

Good night and God bless, for may the God-ness of the day stay with you. The universe is a friend…

Always XXX

THE ONE ROAD (Return to the Godhead)

Basic Principles For The Living.

1: Meditate for 3 minutes a day Am & Pm and send out prayers for the good of all in the world.
Once mastered…

2: Meditate for 15 minutes a day Am & Pm and send out prayers for the good of all in the world.
Once mastered…

3: Meditate for 30 minutes a day Am & Pm and send out prayers for the good of all in the world.
Once mastered…

4: Meditate for 1 hour a day Am & Pm and send out prayers for the good of all in the world.
Once mastered…

5: Meditate, Pray, Walk and Eat in silence for one day in an arranged hermitage or another safe place within a place of nature.
Once mastered…

6: Meditate, Pray, Walk and Eat in silence for one day a month for 12 months in an arranged hermitage or another safe place in nature.
Once mastered…

7: Meditate, Pray, Walk and Eat in silence for four weeks duration with weekends off… in an arranged hermitage or another safe place.
Once mastered…

8: Meditate, Pray, Walk and Eat in silence for forty days duration with weekends off… in an arranged hermitage or another safe place. Go "Within" and learn to Know Thyself Well.

9: Speak of all men, women, children, animals including yourself with Respect, Love, Kindness and Compassion always.

10: Treat all men, women, children, and animals, including yourself with Respect, Love, Kindness and Compassion always, as you like to receive.

11: Be Grateful - For everything, every experience of life, for it will teach you something, as you are a student of living.

12: Change your attitude to positive, see the good and the beauty that surrounds you and if you cannot, then look harder for it is hiding in the illusion right under your very noses.

13: Look in the mirror every day and be honest with yourselves about all things and all situations to the best of your ability, really look.

14: Look in the mirror every day and see your inner beauty, the light, tell yourself you are beautiful and that you love you, in your authenticity for you were created in such richness in the image and the likeness of God.

15: If you see a man, woman, child, or animal in 'poverty' and you have more, share, do what you can. For a little act of unconditional love and kindness goes a long way in the heart of all.

16: If you see a man, woman, child or animal in 'suffering' in any way, then do what you can. For a little act of unconditional love and kindness goes a long way in the hearts of all.

17: Respect and love all that follow all faiths and philosophies, as they return to source the same as you. Do not be the Judge and the Jury, for only Christ knows the truth that lies within one's heart, as we will all reach the same 'Gateway' to the God Head in LOVE.

18: Respect and love all cultures, as the soul signature does not have a different accent or colour to yours. For we are all the same within and travel, our own authentic paths of learning, back home to the God Head, as we should all be living and acting in goodness always, as no harm should ever be done to another.

19: Live in the here and now, in the present for we cannot alter the past or the future as it has not yet arrived. So live in the present, the most precious GIFT... the gift of life.

20: Do not entertain negative thoughts such as Jealousy... for this is harmful to all in the consciousness. Plant only good seeds into your private garden. Weed daily and burn the weeds in the inner flame, the white fire of purity, see them wither away as they go up in smoke, over and over again as necessary, until they are no more for they can be destroyed in love.

21: Finally, FORGIVE... For they know not what they do, including you.

2 plus 1 = 3 The Holy Spirit, the Trinity LOVE

UNIVERSAL PRAYER

Our Father whose heart is love.
God shall always be thy name.
Thy Kingdom come.
Thy will be done.
On Earth as it is in Heaven.
For As above As below, As within As without.
Give us this day our daily abundance.
And Forgive us… our trespasses
As we have forgiven ourselves & all those… who have trespassed
against us.
We shall not walk into temptation, as our hearts shall remain
protected from all darkness.
For MINE is the kingdom, the power and the glory.
Forever and Ever.
In Gratitude.
OM……

AMEN.

CONCLUSION/RE-ENTRY

Good Morning and may the God-ness of the day be with you as the universe is a friend.

I am not writing each day as I did before on my 40 days, as I can see already how the world impacts and how I have allowed it to invade my space. The family is moving houses, big life changes and a poorly little one, so much to get done and assistance to be given. Losing myself already in the illusion of others lives. But unconditional love means sometimes placing yourself to one side while helping to tend to the needs of those you love. A few days and I am back at my special place, so for now it is okay as I give myself permission, as I can balance. So with a few visits to the Garden Station, walks alone in the park and meditation; as this will help me to stay where it needs to be, in love… and peace, centred.

A talk was held yesterday as it had been booked previously and as I spoke I watched the eyes, the gateway to the soul, some unsure, others open, for some knew me before and already trusted. I watched the room as realisation occurred, as issues from childhood rose to the surface and loss on many levels, as tears and laughter both flow from their hearts… The longer I speak, the more they see and begin to feel… in their process of healing.

A friend's name was mentioned whom I know well and how lovely I thought as she too has helped them. Remember to replace that Rose Quartz Crystal I say, for self-love is required first and foremost. You are the most important person in this room… YOU… all of you as individuals. And as I talk about the tools in my tool kit, not just one but many in my Mary Poppins Bag. They realise that we are all unique and may need this one today but another tomorrow, for never are we always the same, as we are ever changing. 'Jack of all trades and master of none' No just a different tool may be required for each and every one of you, as you are not a round peg trying to fit into a square hole.

So use all that you can to assist yourself and eat your fill, for we do not eat just 'one food'. We taste from many and benefit from the richness of the greatest soup. 18 vegetables are far better than just a tomato... how much nourishment we will be receiving if we all link into everything that life has to offer. Taste the Earth's glory, explore and experience all of its foods and its beauty, for today is another day. Another moment, another opportunity... Do not let it just become a memory that fades but 'live'. Truly live in it all and its entirety.

Happy smiling faces leave the hall and I am truly grateful to have met new people yet again and have been in service. For there is nothing more rewarding than this when working in love with an open heart, connecting with others and helping them to begin...to heal their pain. 'We are not our story' as I reiterate with my talk... We really are not! Funny how I can feel the pace of the world, stress and tension as I have allowed it to seep in my body, as a noticing occurs... and I am holding my shoulders up to my ears. Let go and breathe Tracy, release for it does not serve you.

For I am human too and I am a work in progress; as you are too always... The most obvious thing for me in regards to re-entry is the lack of nature, not hearing the dawn chorus from here and not smelling the grass, the flowers, while feeling the freshness of the morning air upon my skin. Also the pace, the chaos as people rush to work on autopilot... with busy minds and busy lives distracted from their soul, their true calling. It is probably shouting...as loud as it can but it cannot be heard, for it is lost somewhere in the illusion of life, its problems and its so-called necessities.

For the expression to not see the wood from the trees is so apt, time out is needed regularly to first of all see and then to know thyself well before the truth can come dancing forth.

For each will have a different version, a different space to fill in the universe for uniqueness is our greatest gift and that is what makes it such a rich and rewarding a plan. Gods plan for all of us… to fill our place to the brim and then more will be given in goodness. A song keeps fleeting through today, I think it is being given to me as a message, about receiving love into my life in all forms; as it has been playing over and over… on and off on repeat since this morning.

I shall not read into anything but just allow it to unfold, as the plan may not yet be fully aligned. So I acknowledge its message and then it disappears; so it must have been for me to take notice…as then another appears 'You gotta have faith'. Do not try to figure anything out; Tracy just allows it all. As when we think, it is like tightness appears around the head, but when inflow outside of ego, it seems to swell from the heart and is wonderful especially when you see it occur in manifestation on earth. The 'Joy' as I arrive to help my ex-husband unpack in his new home, it feels so peculiar because this was my old home, a place where I had taken sanctuary before my leaving the area for Essex. His new home, my old one, how odd… yet so right for him! As he will be safe here surrounded by old friends.

A place for him to settle for the first time in many years and a place of his own, for he has never yet lived alone. This will be a training ground, his place of peace, for growth and to start a new for it is never too late.

I am receiving messages from people who are viewing the videos of this book, and I just want to say thank you for it is truly humbling when people say I want some of what you have! Can you show me what is it that you do differently from me...I remember feeling similar to this myself when I sought out role models and speakers for my own self-development. The responsibility however, belongs to us for no one can be our rescuer, only us. Something is happening in my energy field during my start of re-entry as I am waking up with the strong waves again, not just first thing but throughout the day with breaks in between. I do not feel this is coming from within unless it is the universe adjusting and turning as it can, or could it be my soul speaking with another, a match, as it seeks itself.

The heart beats wildly again and takes my breath away, so I decided to meditate with assistance from Sai Baba today. As I listen to the words, the tears flow... not in crying as I have said before but in the soul, for it is not a cry of emotion; but a cry from the heart of unconditional love, as it feels its truth so beautiful as the water gently rolls... down the cheeks in slow motion. The music draws it forth further and further and the feeling of ecstasy and bliss are overflowing as I control my breath and stay centred in peace, the divinity.

Today is another day... in contrast to yesterday, for all night I have tossed and turned as though someone is in distress and it brings me to tears. I awake with the feeling of uneasiness, is this someone close to me who I know, I wonder for why I am picking this up in the consciousness. I feel pulled to make contact to discover where but my dream reminds me to mind my own, they will contact me if help is required for it is their responsibility and their learning. I put on my phone and internet and the universe sends me signals, messages of an unfolding, so I am going into prayer and silence to send healing for it is needed today.

Tomorrow I am going back into the sanctuary where this all started wow over six weeks ago, six wonderful weeks, the best of my life within the shed in the woods. Two weeks have passed in much of a blur as the outside world has pushed and pulled. People needing assistance and my energy being taken, I have had judgments galore and advice for how I should be living… lol… it's amazing how others wish you to remain the same for they are safe and familiar. I have been too busy and need to rest more as the body is tightening, all the muscles are on full alert informing me that I am doing too much for others and must put myself first. I have also been mulling over the use of the 'I' as in the self and ego… as God stated "I Am all that I am" so now I do not feel so bothered about its use, as I feel I know myself well and will not accept my ego to override my knowing.

'I am' is used in many affirmations… I am healthy to manifest goodness into our lives in every way, so I will continue to use this as it has served me well along with my intuition. The days have been lovely here; a relief in a way yet also the shed is calling me and the peace of the woods, as even now a rural home is louder than nature.

What a change has occurred as previously this beautiful home felt like I was in the middle of nowhere and now although still home I realise I am still somewhere in the world closer… to people and more easily accessible for their needs and wants. The thought of withdrawing further into nature takes hold of me and I let go to allow the energy through, I do not know how this will occur but I know that it will as I can feel it within. My ex-husband is offering space at his home, as he feels I am still homeless... yet this is not really only part of the illusion, so this is not necessary.

As I am writing this now from further within the heart of Northumberland, in a place surrounded by forest, I realise this space is required more than ever, as the writing occurs when I am alone and can hear nothing but silence and the birds.

It is 7 am and the sun is shining, I am sitting out in the garden with a view of the forest and the surrounding area, no sounds at all apart from the songs of the birds, as beautiful as they all serenade me. My awareness shifts and I can feel the deer watching me from the depths of the trees, for their energy is linking with mine; the earth appears to breathe as I watch it intently and a mist swirls around my face, the veil...so thin into other worlds.

It is beautiful to ground myself to the core of the earth and to also connect to the divinity of the consciousness in the universe, as I hold my stone embedded with a silver cross from a special place and my white one from an Essex beach in the shape and sculpture of a feather. I can see and feel the animals before they appear before me as I see a rabbit in my mind's eye and then he comes hopping out of the trees towards me, I laugh and smile as I watch with delight such a sight.

My awareness shifts and a memory triggers of Swami and his message as he said, when you are on your travels Tracy look for a home, a place to call your own where people can visit. I look around me as this place is so calm and wonder, do I resonate more with nature or the sea as the ebb and the flow is within, or both? We shall see what occurs.

As the sun comes out further and the warmth of its rays caresses my skin... surely life cannot get better than this as this is pure bliss. Breakfast is eaten in silence, listening to nature and then a friend arrives, she proceeds to sit beside me and as we chat, the story of the tree at the bottom of the garden is told. It is beautiful I say, as I gaze lovingly at its leaves in its splendour, yes she replies it is a silver birch tree. Oh, how wonderful I exclaim, as I love the spiritual significance of Silver Birch, and the spiritual teachings, and as I gaze further within its branches, I notice it is a twin top, with that I say quickly...It is a twin top silver birch spiritually significant and then we laugh as my relaxer chair suddenly shoots me back in the lying position.

We are hysterical...as even she states at the exact same time, I wonder if that is symbolic Lol...I wonder who is on the way! She gets all excited and says that would be wonderful, a lovely match for you and for us to go out with too, from time to time. I think...these people are here to stay somehow, as they are so kind and sweet... wanting the absolute best for me in every way, I am so blessed.

Her husband then emerges with three homemade juices in hand, full of nutrition and goodness, kale, carrots, orange, apple, banana and more, such are the friends that I adore, I am so grateful that the universe brought us together... so grateful. The day today has unfolded well and it has been truly wonderful as I retire to bed and begin to drift, when suddenly an energy invades my space and my whole body jerks... the waves begin, and I relax as I let go allowing them to explore and sink into my heart... as I know who this is and they mean no harm. I have awoken this morning in fear of a remembrance of a dream, it is 5am and I have allowed it to enter my energy field for I can feel my whole body tightening and my breath shallow for I have become fearful for another.

As I look at the dream, I know this is not for me but that of my dear friend who is linking into my energy, as the last two nights they have entered my dreams, for they are feeling alone and mistakenly abandoned by me, I send out prayers immediately with much love and compassion for their lessons are theirs alone and if we do not all take responsibility then our tests will not be known. The tightening eases as I send out so much love, for this is truly given and then I rest again in the knowledge that they are capable… they can do this.

At 7.00 I decided to go downstairs and meditate in the garden, as the sun is rising, the birds are singing, a woodpecker here is working as I can hear his drill and the view breathtaking, so I re-enter my place of peace to set myself up for the day ahead, as my life is mine and needs the same love and care as I send out to others.

A decision is made to practice love and compassion for myself and I search within for the fragments of fear which may still be hiding, soon they are shown, so I bring them into full awareness. As I view the issues, I then pull them both gently into the Grace of the heart, observing… as they dissolve in the love of the Christ consciousness… The divine love of Grace and I feel the softness of the energy as it ebbs and flows through this sacred space… release… releasing myself from anything that no longer serves me.

The sun has now moved around and warms my face, as I relax further and observe myself joined…on the thread of God's Love, for I am supported, cared for and always loved as we are never separate from the whole.

As I open my eyes, I gaze at the time and already 1 hour 20 minutes have passed…how can that be? As once 3 minutes felt like an eternity. Discipline Tracy, always discipline…as it serves you well, so I decide to go back into practice but with dance, as I dance in the garden in a trance, connected to the grass as my feet are bare grounding my energy in nature.

Such is the feeling of peace as after a while I complete my practice, by standing in stillness… as within as without, with my right palm facing down towards the earth and the left one facing up to the sky balance. As above as below remain in flow… do not allow the outside world to distract you from the truth of love. I move location to another place, 40 miles away today, still rural and peaceful, and another beautiful sanctuary.

Another day has come forth and this time I feel the energy of despair… for something is clearing but it is not gentle, it is reaching me with such a force that it is taking my breath away… is this mine, I wonder or another invasion of my space. My physical body is struggling to cope with the impact and now I want to give up… to give up on all my dreams, my hopes and my destiny, for this is torture! It is like being loved and despised at the same time…it rips you apart and then as you fall into a place of deep peace it starts again, such is the torment.

I walk into the bathroom and see a vision of someone doing the same and as you walk around the room in synchronicity, I see who this is why can you not leave me alone? Is it because you are me? And I am you? If so then make yourself known!! Where art thou and why then have you not made contact? If you feel this pain and this depth of the pure divine love.

You have invaded my dreams for many nights now as I saw you in one, on fire… and now you invade my waking hour… I try to move forward and then I am pulled back, like a magnet to your heart, so I sit in the space of unconditional love and dissolve any difficulties in the heart of all hearts… of Grace. On and off… all day it has been like this, as the internal waves have gained in strength, as you have walked a past path in memory.

So, again and again I have cleared the space, sending love, to allow new energy to rise like a new dawn, yet still, you pull it back… Let go, I say… Let go. I can feel your desire and your depth of love, so be it then, I scream as I surrender, for I cannot sleep or rest or work… so I pray and pray again for this to pass.

I fetch my beautiful Tibetan Mala beads and chant… as the Absolute is real and I am the student of this greatest teacher, for I am rare, I know my worth and I will not be deterred from my spiritual path, you are welcome to join me at anytime but I will never be taken away from the truth. I am as precious a gift like the rarest of diamonds… I know this now… This too shall pass I whisper to myself, this too shall pass. At 9pm I lay exhausted on my bed and finally fall asleep, as the feeling of the connection takes place the connection between us… of all the chakras coming into my awareness, as the vibration, the tingling of the energy, the spinning of the wheels, from the earth star to the top of my crown and above… I close my eyes and sink into the energy as it is peaceful.

What now I say as I am awoken yet again with a dream for it is like a yo-yo. Make a decision for goodness sake, I say… either leave or come forth, for I am prepared to stay and will always speak with you, as there is nothing that cannot be resolved in loving kindness and compassion. So I pull a couple of cards and they say Destiny and Time Out...I am reassured... nothing to be done... so I go back to sleep for tomorrow is a new day; and I am hoping with all hope that you are busy/distracted in the world and not able to think... for I too need to work on my plans, for my future and my love for all.

Since leaving the shed, I have seen much and learnt so much more, as we are always the student and the teacher, for in my own realisation... I too, have seen others and where they are struggling to see within themselves and they are truly suffering. A tortured soul comes to me for assistance and I give it with unconditional love but after a couple of treatments, I feel she needs more of another therapy, for I can only deal with certain aspects and I am not trained in the specialist area of the mind.

I can assist from the place of my own training, my own skills, my experience and learning, on both a professional and spiritual level but she needs another type of professional who can help her with the mind and her thinking, for this is impacting upon her behaviour and her life as she is not receiving the goodness.

So I will refer her to another...

From this place of understanding, I know now that I can support many to find this, as I know how it works and how you can reach an inner state of connection with yourself in the truth of love. Once you begin to clear away the parts that no longer serve you. The responsibility for change is ours, each of us as individuals and we have to be honest with ourselves in every way.

As we begin to look deep within and see the reasons why, what, where and how things have occurred for us in our lifetime, for it is only then can start to be free... This starting point will be the stumbling block for many... as they do not wish to see the truth of themselves, as it is a choice - a choice that it is often not made, for it is easier to stay in the illusion in a place of the safe and the familiar... .The hamster wheel, as they go round and round and round... It may appear confusing... but really it is not, it is simple.

KISS: Keep it simple sweetheart... just undo everything and start again in the truth. As I conclude this book I know this is not the end... it may be the completion of the 40 Days and 40 Nights in silence, 'within' the shed in the woods but this is really only the beginning of a new chapter and book three is starting already in earnest. As my journey has been walking back to happiness... that song from the south pacific, it is wonderful... as it is truly 'Heaven on Earth.'

I send the readers of this book so many blessings of Love & Light... Laughter, Health and Prosperity! For I wish everyone the same as I wish for myself.

All my love... from the Grace of the heart, the beloved.

Always Tracy. X

FOR YOU TO WRITE YOUR NOTES

FOR YOU TO WRITE YOUR NOTES

45916780R00160

Printed in Poland
by Amazon Fulfillment
Poland Sp. z o.o., Wrocław